MINDFULNESS EXERCISES
For Kids

75 EASY RELAXATION TECHNIQUES TO HELP YOUR CHILD FEEL BETTER

LILIAN FORSTER

© Copyright 2020 by Lilian Forster. All right reserved.

The work contained herein has been produced with the intent to provide relevant knowledge and information on the topic described in the title for entertainment purposes only. While the author has gone to every extent to furnish up to date and true information, no claims can be made as to its accuracy or validity as the author has made no claims to be an expert on this topic. Notwithstanding, the reader is asked to do their research and consult any subject matter experts they deem necessary to ensure the quality and accuracy of the material presented herein.

This statement is legally binding as deemed by the Committee of Publishers Association and the American Bar Association for the territory of the United States. Other jurisdictions may apply their legal statutes. Any reproduction, transmission, or copying of this material contained in this work without the express written consent of the copyright holder shall be deemed as a copyright violation as per the current legislation in force on the date of publishing and subsequent time after that. All additional works derived from this material may be claimed by the holder of this copyright.

The data, depictions, events, descriptions, and all other information forthwith are considered to be true, fair, and accurate unless the work is expressly described as a work of fiction. Regardless of the nature of this work, the Publisher is exempt from any responsibility of actions taken by the reader in conjunction with this work. The Publisher acknowledges that the reader acts of their own accord and releases the author and Publisher of any responsibility for the observance of tips, advice, counsel, strategies, and techniques that may be offered in this volume.

TABLE OF CONTENTS

Preface 7

Introduction 10

Chapter 1: A Peaceful Mind 14
    1) Best Day Ever Contemplation 17
    2) Deep Breathing Friend 18

Chapter 2: Emotional Awareness 22
    3) Designing a Face 22
    4) Anger Buster Meditation 25
    5) Notecard Journal 29
    6) Emotional Charades 31
    7) Emotional Escape Meditation 32
    8) Contemplation on Perspective 34
    9) Positive Affirmation Anchor 37

Chapter 3: Anti-Anxiety 42
    10) Peaceful Breathing 42
    11) Easy Counting 43
    12) A Beautiful Flower 44

13) Rabbit Nosed 44
14) A Snake's Hiss 45
15) 3-4-3 45
16) Wave Breathing 46
17) Hand Breathing 46
18) Quick Exercises 47
19) Embrace Yourself 47
20) Earmuffs 47
21) Holding a Hand 48
22) Grateful Hand 48
23) Grounding Stone. 48
24) Stress Ball 49
25) A Sunny Meditation 50
26) Learning to Focus for Meditation 53
27) A Quick Meditation for Relaxation 54
28) Glitter Jar Stress Tool 56
29) Relaxation Stretching 58
30) Cat Scratch Stretching 58
31) Downward Dog 59
32) Back and Leg Stretch 59

Chapter 4: Concentration 62

33) The Bell 62
34) The Pinpoint 63
35) Mystery Bag 64
36) Leaves and Details 66
37) Drawing Your Breath 68
38) A Concentration Game 69
39) Screen Meditation 71

40) The Amazing Apple 72
41) Distraction 74

Chapter 5: Observation 77

42) Super Senses 77
43) Bonus Round! 79
44) What is the Point of This? 79
45) Three Changes 80
46) Matching Game 82
47) Long Term Observation 84
48) Scavenger Hunt 86
49) Quiet Time 87
50) Texture Crafting 88
51) The Colored Card Game 90
52) Cup Game 92
53) Observational Meditation 93

Chapter 6: Visualization 98

54) Enchanted Forest 98
55) Picture of Paradise (Optional) 101
56) A Meadow in Springtime 102
57) Butterfly Garden 105
58) Picture of My Wings 110
59) Cabin Meditation 111
60) Spirit Creature 113
61) Picture of Your Guardian (Optional) 116

Chapter 7: Body and Senses 119

62) Beating Heart 119
63) Flamingo 121

64) STOP 123
65) Taste Test 124
66) Brave Old World 126
67) Red Light Green Light 127
68) Obstacle Course 128
Yoga for Children 130
69) Prayer Pose 130
70) Chair Pose 130
71) Lunge Pose 131
72) Warrior Pose 131
73) Warrior II 131
74) Body Acceptance Craft 131
75) A Thank You Note (Meditation) 134

Conclusion **137**

PREFACE

In *Mindfulness Exercises for Kids: 75 Relaxation Techniques to Help Your Child Feel Better,* parents and teachers will find a plethora of useful exercises meant to encourage children's mental health. This book is a resource for anyone who spends time with kids and is invested in their success. Stability, awareness, positive self-esteem, and emotional growth may be achieved through mindfulness, especially when the individual learns these habits early.

Is your child stressed out? Do they have a difficult time conveying their emotions or empathizing with the feelings of others? Research has shown that meditation and mindfulness in schools drastically reduce aggression in children. Can you imagine the benefits of bringing these exercises home? Even your child's concentration and observational skills will improve.

Childhood is already challenging; there are so many new and conflicting expectations from parents, teachers, and peers. Teach your little ones to understand their own desires and feelings so that they are not lost in the noise. Children also benefit from learning to manage difficult emotions when they do arise. Growth and progress are possible when learning is made more digestible. These exercises are a blast for kids, all while teaching them the skills they need for a happy life.

What is mindfulness? Do you need healing crystals and a personal spiritual advisor? Nope. As it turns out, mindfulness is a practical term for finding calm through being present in the moment and accepting yourself. True peace can be vital during the storms that tend to arise throughout our lives. Teaching these skills to children is beyond beneficial for their mental health. Imagine developing habits that could have saved you heartbreak during your hormonal teenage years. Imagine having the emotional stability to love yourself as an adult, without ever having to buy another self-help book.

Reading this book you're going to find out all of the fundamental ways that mindfulness can improve your child's life now and later! Your little one will learn about their own emotions and how to understand the feelings of others. Kids perform exercises that foster feelings of self-love. Young minds soak up new habits that change their concentration and improve the way they observe the world. Watch how much detail your child notices after just a few of these activities.

- Children learn to thrive, even in challenging situations. Self-soothing techniques ensure that your little one is always comforted, even when you are not around. Your little ones will learn the basics of meditation, visualization, and breath control.

- Concentration skills are improved as children are challenged through games, crafts, meditations, and experiments.

PREFACE

- Watch as your child learns new ways to process the world around them with all of their senses with activities that they will want to repeat again and again.

- Create an environment where your children are comfortable being open and honest with you as they begin to explore their own feelings and developing personality.

- Give your child a better understanding of how their body works through exercises that test balance and test physical observations.

INTRODUCTION

Thank you so much for your purchase of *Mindfulness Exercises for Kids: 75 Relaxation Techniques to Help Your Child Feel Better*. This book exists to help children become well-versed in mindfulness. Scientific research has shown that kids exposed to meditation and mental health exercises are more emotionally intelligent than average. Through the activities inside of this book, children will learn to love and accept themselves while maintaining an affection for the world they occupy.

In 2011 one of the most influential studies sought to determine the usefulness of teaching mindfulness practices to children. This study was one of the largest of its kind, taking place thanks to a collaboration between Mindful Schools (a research group) and the University of California, Davis. Nine hundred thirty-seven children participated in the project, and the results were promising (fig 1).

Educators took a course that enabled them to embed mindful practices into the curriculum. Students in the control group were offered a tiny taste of mindfulness through a four-hour instructional lesson. Children who were exposed to the change in their entire

INTRODUCTION

syllabus showed significant signs of improvement in areas related to concentration, compassion, and engagement.

Researchers with Mindful Schools are hopeful about the outcome of their study. The more children are immersed in mindful practices, the better their scholastic experience. Mindful Schools is confident that their courses will continue to foster improvement in academic institutions and even offer online options for teachers.

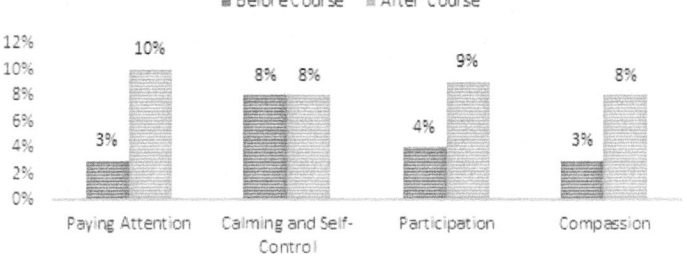

Fig 1. Behavioral improvement of children when exposed to the mindful curriculum (6 Weeks), 2011-2012 Graph from Mindful Schools, Mindful Schools. Web. 17 Sept. 2020. n.pag.

Childhood is already challenging; kids take in so much new information while also attempting to navigate their desires and impulses. New schedules, fragile friendships, family life, expectations in the classroom, and so many factors compound to place pressure on children. Without the tools to navigate emotional obstacles, little ones sometimes find themselves feeling lost and confused. This book is full of exercises that address emotion, tension, concentration, and more.

Mindfulness even has a hand in the development of a child's imagination. Meditation and visualization exercises carry your little one off to faraway lands while imparting essential lessons. Watch your children's progress as they learn to dream with all of their senses and better interpret abstract concepts.

Being present in the moment and accepting one's environment and oneself is a massive piece of the mindfulness puzzle. The exercises inside this book seek to help children reach this goal. Emotional awareness and thoughtful reactions make a vast difference in maturity, even when a young mind is still developing. There are so many excellent mindfulness books on the market; thank you again for choosing this one.

Chapter 1
A Peaceful Mind

CHAPTER 1

A PEACEFUL MIND

If you were to divide the human lifespan into different phases based upon the changing objectives relative that time in their lives, an informative picture would take shape. The earliest years of our lives are incredibly important for determining the direction of attitude, morals, stability, and learning capabilities. Infancy and early childhood are the foundation upon which we build.

Nurturing a child's curiosity in the world around them is paramount for preserving a little piece of that intense imagination for the coming years. Teaching your little one the importance of mindfulness can afford them the tools to handle life's more difficult hurdles. Self-soothing is a skill that will propel through some of the darkest days ahead by helping to regulate challenging emotions.

Babies and infants depend upon their parents for every need. What if you could use this time to impart behaviors that allowed the child to find comfort and peace on their own? Through the use of mindfulness exercises, you can ensure that your child can pull from their own experience to solve challenging problems.

A PEACEFUL MIND

Mindfulness is a peaceful mental state reached through relaxation and practice, a marriage of the mind with the moment. Feelings, thoughts, and sensations no longer hold the individual captive. All parts of the self are accepted and acknowledged without being grated control.

It is through mindfulness that children can learn to weather difficult situations and quell anxiety. Learning these techniques in one's youth makes peace much more comfortable to achieve into adulthood. Throughout this book, you will find exercises that teach this meditative state of mind in a way that children can digest.

Inner peace is something that humans seem to struggle with more and more, as our technology advances. Each new generation is exposed to additional information; more images and words than someone living a hundred years ago would see in their entire lifetime. The price for progress is a growing epidemic of stress and tension.

Making meditation and mindfulness digestible is imperative for the mental health of the next generation. We must all work together to ensure that the youth have the knowledge they need to combat the rising mental health crisis. Finding peace is vital for living a long and happy life.

Studies have shown that mindfulness training can improve learning environments for those with mental illnesses and learning disabilities. Children that would otherwise prove unable to form a connection are bonding with their peers. Learning to manage feelings and impulses productively and positively will likely become a part of the curriculum in the not so distant future.

Sometimes it is difficult to remember the stresses of childhood, but your little one is busy discovering so many new things. School, friends, schedules, family life, practices, and so many other factors compound to put pressure on kids while their world is already changing so quickly. Mindfulness offers a moment of respite while relieving stress and teaching good habits that will help for years to come.

Throughout this book, children will learn to calm themselves down during intense situations, cope with intense emotions, develop their observational skills, understand and love their bodies, and fine-tune their senses. Kids respond to different things, so this book features a variety of exercises. Little ones will be able to try out so many types of activities to find what works for them.

Mindfulness is about understanding one's own thoughts, feelings, and actions in a positive way. Learning these skills early in life has been shown to alter the thinking of an individual for the rest of their life. Brain imaging has suggested that using exercises linked to mindfulness can strengthen the cerebral cortex.

Children who work on their awareness change their brain structure to become better at reasoning and problem-solving. Mindfulness also relieves stress and anxiety. The mind is so powerful that schools who engage in mindfulness training have seen a decrease in behaviors related to bullying. Individuals who have a better and more positive understanding of their emotions do not perpetuate aggressive behaviors toward peers.

We will begin our journey with a few easy exercises that both you and your young participants may appreciate!

1) BEST DAY EVER CONTEMPLATION

THE SCRIPT:

I would like for you to take a moment to shake the extra energy from your hands and fingers, and then close your eyes. Take a moment to scan your brain; I want you to think of the best day of your young life so far. Try to remember what you were doing during this time.

Answer the following questions quietly, to yourself:

- What was I doing on this day?
- Why was I so happy?
- What else was I feeling?
- What was the weather/temperature like on this day?
- Do I remember any sensations? Did I touch anything?
- What were the smells present during this day?
- If I could go back to this time, what would I hear?
- Did I taste anything that day?

Perhaps your most favorite memory is a pool party that you had for your birthday, one year. Recall the way the chlorine tasted when you jumped into the chilly water; remember how it burned your eyes. The other children were laughing and yelling, a sound which distorted as you sank below the surface of the liquid.

That scene is just one example, and your own will be completely different. Activities like this exercise our senses so that we can use them even in our imagination. Remembering moments with such detail will also better preserve the memories in our minds and encourage us to notice details during observation.

2) DEEP BREATHING FRIEND

Deep Breathing Friend is a crafting exercise that is going to allow the participating children to use their artistic skills! The creation that you will have made by the end of this activity will teach little ones how to breathe deeply. So many meditations and calming techniques require a particular method of inhaling and exhaling.

You are going to cut a hole in the bottom platform of a paper cup, about the size of a quarter. The different colored tissue paper will be cut into long strips and attached to the open end of the cup (opposite from the incision). The children participating in this activity will breathe in deeply, through their nose, and then breathe out through the hole that you cut. The air passing through the tube will cause the streamers to dance as the children watch their craft come to life.

MATERIALS NEEDED:

- Paper cups
- Tissue paper (fun colors)
- Crafting razor or scissors (for you)
- Glue
- Markers

A PEACEFUL MIND

- Googly eyes (optional)
- Pipe cleaners, pom poms, glitter, and other craft decorations (optional)

INSTRUCTIONS:

1. Set out enough paper cups for the exercise. There should be one cup for every child participating in the activity.
2. Cut a hole the size of a quarter (or a little larger) into the bottom of every paper cup before the activity begins. The hole should be made on the small flat end, where the cup would sit upon a surface. You are turning the cup into a tube, through which air may flow.
3. Give each kid a cup and a few markers so that they can decorate the outside. They may choose to make their cup into an animal, or they could just draw on the outside of it.
4. The tissue paper is going to be cut into long strips.
    a. Less than an inch thick and around four inches long is recommended.
5. Place a little glue on one of the short edges of each streamer.
6. Adhere the tissue streamer to the inside of the cup, right at the open edge.
    a. If you were to turn your paper cup upside down, it would look like an octopus with all of the streamers hanging out of the larger opening.

7. Instruct children to deeply inhale through their nose and then exhale through the smaller hole in the cup (the one you cut). The streamers on the other end will dance in the air as the children breathe out.

Note: Keep an eye on the deep breathing to make sure that the children do not cause themselves to hyperventilate. Should you ever witness hyperventilation, have the individual breathe out slowly for a few cycles before resuming their natural pattern.

Chapter 2
Emotional Awareness

CHAPTER 2
EMOTIONAL AWARENESS

Emotional awareness can be one of the most challenging areas for a child to master. Human feelings are nuanced, and we do not always say what we mean. Through these exercises, you can teach your child about all of the modes of expression.

Show your child that complex moods are possible. People are all vastly different, and all have varying ways of expressing their feelings to one another; some use their gestures to convey their feelings while others use their voice or their face. Follow some of the exercises below for a fun way to learn about emotions.

3) DESIGNING A FACE

This exercise is aimed at teaching children facial expressions that display emotions and the subtle differences between feelings that might seem similar. Being able to discern other people's moods is a vital piece of the Emotional Awareness puzzle. In this activity, you and the children work together to learn a fun lesson.

EMOTIONAL AWARENESS

MATERIALS NEEDED:

You may use whatever materials you have available for this exercise. Painting smooth stones with acrylic could be a wholly separate activity. Pipe cleaners, markers, and construction paper could also be perfect for this exercise. When all else fails, printer paper and crayons/pens/pencils will also work beautifully. Make this exercise your own by finding your own creative style. You will also need a piece of yarn (or string), around three feet long, to form your "head." The yard could be substituted with a bit of paper with an oval drawn upon it.

- Design different facial features (eyes and mouth) on separate pieces of paper. When crafting the eyes, make sure you have a close match. You can use whatever materials you have decided upon for this exercise. Include a few different noses just to have some variation, even though they are not emotionally significant.

- Make a separate set of eyes and a mouth for each of the following significant emotions: happiness, anger, sadness, disgust, fear, and surprise. You can always expand your set of features to include more complex feelings in the future!

- Consider adding in some wildcard features so that the children participating in the lesson have the chance to use their imagination.

- If you are using paper, cut out a separate piece for each eye and mouth. Convey one of the above expressions to the best of your artistic ability. If your child is old enough to help, engage them in the drawing/painting process. Do not worry

- about your own skill level in this activity; simple eyes are just as valuable as detailed eyes.

- Making the features wild, colorful, and goofy can help ensure that you keep your little one's attention throughout the exercise. Decorating your creations can also be a fun bonding craft for you and your child.

- Once your features have been created and you are ready to begin the exercise, use the yarn/string to form an oval on the floor. This is going to serve as the head, upon which the two of you will place your features.

- When the exercise commences, take turns so that your little one better understands how to complete their own masterpiece.

INSTRUCTIONS:

1. Take turns crafting a unique face with the available features. Instruct the participating children to form their own expressions by placing two eyes, a nose, and a mouth inside the oblong oval shape that has been laid out upon the work surface with yarn

2. Have the children explain the emotion they were trying to convey with the features that they used.

    a. Correct any misunderstanding while still allowing for creativity. A frown used to convey happiness would be incorrect but angry eyes could still illustrate disgust. Use your better judgment when explaining inaccuracies.

EMOTIONAL AWARENESS

    b. The corrections should be made without discouraging abstract thinking. If the child can justify their use of a feature for a particular emotion, then their answer can be considered accurate.

3. Ask the participating children to come up with a sentence for their expression. When I feel (emotion displayed), I_____. The statement should explore the emotion they illustrated along with the reaction they experience in their body, from the feeling. Asking the children to analyze their emotions and responses gives them the chance to consider the way feelings manifest in the physical body.

    a. When I feel **angry**, I **stomp**.

    b. When I feel **sad, I cry**.

4) ANGER BUSTER MEDITATION

Emotions are powerful; they have so much influence over our actions. Even adults have difficulties when it comes to regulating negative feelings and the way we react to unpleasant situations. This exercise is going to include a quick and versatile meditation that may be taught to children and called upon whenever they feel frustrated, mad, or upset.

    Meditation is such an imperative tool for mindfulness and can allow us access to the parts of our own brain that we would otherwise never visit. It is through these sorts of activities that we learn about mental and emotional health. Expressing feelings, even the unfun ones, in a constructive way, can change the way we react during intense situations.

Find a quiet room where you and your audience will be able to relax. Before the meditation begins, allow the children to dance around for a minute, to relieve any pent-up energy they might have left in their limbs. Instruct the participating children to sit with their legs crossed in front of them; their hands may rest upon their laps in a comfortable position.

You will be reading the meditation from a script as the children close their eyes and follow along with your voice. The exercise may be repeated whenever your child feels upset or angry. Eventually, the words will become ingrained in the minds of the participants, and they may use the activity on their own to self-soothe.

THE SCRIPT:

Close your eyes, and begin gently taking deep breaths in and out. Inhale through your nose and exhale through your mouth, holding the air inside your chest and belly for just a moment. Deep breathing should be comfortable, so do not overextend yourself; you are telling your brain that you want to relax.

As you continue breathing in and out, listen to the sound that the air makes as it travels through your body. Pay attention to the noise in your nose as you drag-in your breath from outside. Feel the expansion of your chest and tummy as you continue to inhale. Feel the sensation in your body as you exhale through your mouth.

EMOTIONAL AWARENESS

We are going to take a couple more deep breaths together, and then you are going to return to your regular breathing pattern. Inhale through your nose and then release the air in a steady stream through your mouth. You are doing such a good job so far.

You can now breathe like you usually do, no more deep breaths. When we take deep breaths, our lungs are telling our brain that everything is alright. It is a signal that there is nothing wrong, and we are free to relax. The next time you find yourself worrying or getting angry, try finding a place just to sit and breathe deeply for a moment.

Anger is a healthy emotion. When we try to bottle our anger up, it can cause us to react in negative ways. Through learning to express our feelings constructively, we can see that being mad is actually normal.

The next time you are so mad that you want to scream, remember that anger is healthy; it's part of being human. You don't have to pretend that you don't feel angry. We just need to learn how to communicate that emotion without hurting anyone else's feelings.

I want you to imagine that you are standing inside an empty room that is painted in your favorite color. You are the only one in this space, and no one else is going to bother you here. You are free in this place!

I want you to pay attention to the feelings in your body as you stand inside your own room. Do you feel tension or pain in any of your limbs? Does your hand hurt? Does your knee ache? Sometimes our body tries to tell us that we are upset.

Accept these sensations, even if they are unpleasant. This is your chance to pay attention to the message your body is sending you. If you feel any pain, relax the muscle or limb from which that ache is coming. Imagine that you are breathing out the bad feelings when you exhale.

Now I want you to allow your thoughts the chance to make themselves known. If there is anything that you are angry or upset about, those things are going to pop up in your mind now. Take a moment to listen to your mind; wait for your emotions to appear to you.

As you remain standing inside your room (the one painted in your most favorite color), I want you to imagine that you are reaching inside your pocket. You feel something smooth and rubbery. What could that be?

You pull out an empty balloon. Now think about the thing that is making you upset. Allow yourself to feel the emotions. Imagine that all of the unpleasant anger, sadness, or frustration is moving to your lungs.

You are going to blow up your imaginary balloon! All your unpleasant emotions are being breathed out as you continue to inhale and exhale. Concentrate all those bad feelings into your balloon, as you begin to fill it up.

Watch as your balloon grows and grows; it is full of your air and your bad feelings. When all the negative emotions have left your body, tie your imaginary balloon. Feel your entire body relax as you hold the rubber orb in front of you.

This exercise is almost over. There is only one thing left to do, and I bet you have probably guessed what you are supposed to do next. Pop that anger balloon! You can stomp on it; you can use an imaginary needle, you can body slam it. Hear the sound of the balloon bursting in your mind.

Continue to listen to your breath as you slowly open your eyes to rejoin the real world. Do you feel better? Does your body feel more relaxed now that you have popped the balloon?

The next time you feel bad, imagine that you are filling a balloon full of those unfun emotions. You can pop your balloon to ultimately return all that sadness, anger, or frustration back into the air. You should feel relaxed and energized now.

5) NOTECARD JOURNAL

In this exercise, the children are going to be offered a safe and straightforward way to express their emotions constructively. Notecard Journal can be a completely private activity, or you could review their work with them at a later date. Teach your little ones to understand and convey their feelings through art or words.

The notecards feature limited space and will help children to prioritize their thoughts in relation to their feelings. Participants will only be able to select one or two sentences to convey complex emotions and will be forced to think critically about their mood. Teaching children to choose their words carefully can help foster better communication skills.

This activity is going to be similar to a journal for children. If your participants are not old enough to read/write, they may skip the word portion of this activity. You may also change this exercise, in any way, to better fit the children taking part. The lesson should be repeated at least once a week.

MATERIALS NEEDED:

- Pack of notecards.
- Writing utensils (pen, pencil, crayon, etc.).
- One small box or container per child (shoeboxes are perfect).
- If there are multiple children engaged in the activity, one box may be used if each participant is assigned a different colored notecard.
- Tape.

1. Write the date on the notecards at the very bottom.
2. Instruct the child to label the top of the card with an emotion they are feeling right at that moment.
3. The child will write one sentence about their feeling (if they are able to write).
    a. I feel (emotion) because (reason).
4. The participating child will then create a small illustration to go along with their emotion; the picture can be whatever they like, from facial expressions to objects that remind them of their current feelings.
5. Cards will be folded in half and taped before being added to their container.

EMOTIONAL AWARENESS

6. These notecards can be reviewed and reflected upon at a later date of your choosing.

6) EMOTIONAL CHARADES

This exercise would be perfect for multiple participants but may also be played with just you and your child. Charades is a game that allows the contestants to guess the word that one selected individual (at a time) is acting out. Emotional Charades enable the group to assess the feeling that is being communicated.

MATERIALS NEEDED:

- Copied lists of emotions for each participant, or a large posterboard with the emotions written upon it.
- Small slips that feature each emotion written out one time (so that they may be drawn by participants).
- A bowl, jar, or open box for the slips.
- Paper/pencil for scoring.

INSTRUCTIONS:

1. One participant (the actor) at a time will draw a slip with an emotion written upon it.
2. The actor will stand in front of everyone (or just you) and act out the emotion until someone correctly guesses. The correct guesser should either receive a prize (a piece of candy) or a point.

3. No words may be used, but sounds are allowed.
4. The next child in line will act out the emotion they drew in the same way.

Shocked	Tired	Embarrassed	Confused	Frustrated
Fearful	Happy	Silly	Shy	Sick
Excited	Sad	Disappointed	Worried	Bored
Guilty	Angry	Disgusted	Content	Jealous

7) EMOTIONAL ESCAPE MEDITATION

The following exercise is a script that you may read aloud to one or more children. The meditative activity will allow the participants to use their imagination while also achieving a peaceful calm for themselves. The following may be helpful for very stimulating days.

Find a quiet room and instruct participating children to sit with their legs crossed before them, with hands resting comfortably in their laps. Dimming the light may help with their concentration in this exercise. Direct your audience to close their eyes.

THE SCRIPT:

Children feel every emotion with intensity, which can be a gift and a curse. So much magical art and creativity come from young minds but being angry or sad can also be much more impactful. Did you know that *you* could calm yourself down on stressful days?

I would like for you to begin by breathing deeply. Slowly inhale through your nose and hold the air inside your lungs while you count

EMOTIONAL AWARENESS

to three in your head. Gently exhale through your mouth as you listen to the sound of my voice.

Try to direct your attention to the sound of your breath. When your mind wanders, just redirect your thoughts back. Focus on the noise again and try your best to keep your attention centered on the air passing through you.

As I speak, your limbs are feeling heavier and heavier. Pay attention to the areas where your own body meets the floor. Do these areas feel significantly heavier than the rest of your body? Keep listening to the sounds of your breath.

I want you to use your imagination now, think of the most relaxing place in the world. Your space could be a beach with rippling turquoise waves, or it could be in the center of a beautiful forest. Your quiet place could be a field full of cotton candy and lollipops or a room in your house where you feel exceptionally safe.

For the next few minutes, I want you to explore this imaginary place in your mind. Walk around and admire the scenery. Answer these questions quietly, inside your head:

1. What do I see when I look around?
2. How is the weather? Is the air warm? Is it snowing in this world? Can you feel the snow or heat upon your skin?
3. What sounds do you hear? Can you make out the distant cawing of seagulls? Is it absolutely silent? Are there birds chirping all around you?

4. Are there any smells in this place? Does it smell like strawberries or fresh-cut grass? Does the scent of the forest fill your nostrils?

Imagine yourself touching something to engage your senses. Place your palm against a surface in your imaginary world. You could also pick up something from the ground, like sand, a leaf, a stone, a flower, etc., feel the item in your hand. Walk around and explore your world for just a little longer.

This is your place, a place that no one can take away from you. Whenever you are sad or scared, you can come here and spend as much time as you like. You can build onto your world using your imagination.

Whenever you need to escape, find a quiet room, and get comfortable. Listen to your breathing until you find yourself completely relaxed. Slowly imagine your place coming to life in front of you, your own private paradise.

8) CONTEMPLATION ON PERSPECTIVE

This exercise is meant to teach children about the way their actions change other people. One compliment can change the course of a stranger's day. The more compassion that we nurture in children today is the positive change we witness in the world tomorrow.

We are going to begin this exercise like we might start a meditation. Have the participating children sit with their legs crossed, and their eyes closed. Make sure that any extra energy has already been released, so that they may focus on the topic at hand.

EMOTIONAL AWARENESS

THE SCRIPT:

Listen to my voice and the sound of your breath, as we begin. Let your breathing get just a little deeper, inhaling through your nose and exhaling through your mouth. Hold the air inside you for just a few seconds before letting it all go. Feel your body beginning to relax.

Today, we are going to talk about the way our actions and words affect other people. You may not realize it, but you have a really important superpower hidden deep inside. You have the power to change someone else's entire mood with just a few words. Now that you know about your superpowers, you have a huge responsibility to treat others well.

If you have trouble deciding how to behave in any given situation, I want you to think of the way you would want people to treat you. Next time someone wants to borrow a pencil, think of how you would like someone to answer the same question from you. You could be the bright spot in someone else's bad day.

Know that you are entirely safe here at this moment. No one is judging you, and you are allowed to be yourself. I am going to ask you some questions, and I want you to answer them in your mind.

Silently, think of the last person who was mean to you.

- Did their words change your mood?
- Did they make you feel like you weren't good enough or as though you were bothering them?
- What is your impression of this person now?

Now, remember the last time someone complimented you.

- How did that make you feel?
- Did their words bring you joy?
- What is your impression of that person now?

Out of the two different feelings, which one do you want to inspire in others? Do you want them to remember you in a positive way or a negative way?

Now we are going to try something a little more challenging. I want you to think of the last time you were mean to someone else. I know this part may not be fun, but it is essential that you participate. I want you to imagine the conversation from the other person's point of view. Try to place yourself in their shoes.

- How do you think your words or actions made this person feel?
- Was there anything that you could have done differently?
- How do you think they felt when the conversation was over?

From now on, when you are talking to other people, I want you to consider the effect your words are having upon them. Watch the way they respond to you and try to imagine the conversation through their eyes. This is your chance to change people's lives for the better.

This exercise is almost over, and I would like to present you with a challenge. From the moment we finish this activity, you have a clean slate. Before the sun sets this evening, I challenge you to do **three** kind things for someone else. You could complement your parents or give a gift to a friend. Maybe you could spend time with someone

EMOTIONAL AWARENESS

who seems like they might need some companionship. Whatever you choose, it is up to you to complete the task. Use your superpower to place a smile on someone else's face today.

9) POSITIVE AFFIRMATION ANCHOR

Positive affirmations are often mentioned in relation to mindfulness, and not just because they make us feel good. These phrases serve to remind us that we are worthy, even when we don't feel so valuable. Repeating these sentiments can also be grounding.

Moods are like the weather, especially for children. Something urgent and horrible at the moment will soon pass, and the world will become calm again. Help children ground themselves through the intense emotional storms by giving them something positive that they may hold onto, always.

THE SCRIPT:

We have an exceptional exercise today! We are going to create our own anchors. An anchor is a heavy metal object that boats drop into troubled ocean waters. When the metal hits the sand at the bottom of the sea, it ensures that the vessel will not move around (even during a storm).

We can create our own anchors to keep us grounded during intense emotional storms. Our anchor is going to be something positive about us that will always be true. You can pick your anchor phrase from a list or create your own. The words you choose will be written on your page, and then you may decorate the image as you see fit.

Let the words you pick remind you that the bad days will always pass. All the wonderful things that you are, you will always be. Look to this picture the next time you feel like the world is moving out from under you.

MATERIALS NEEDED:

- Paper or notecard.
- Writing utensil.
- Crayons, markers, or colored pencils (optional, but will make the project more fun).
- Transparent packing tape or page protector (optional).

ACTIVITY

1. Draw or print a basic anchor on a notecard or piece of plain paper. Have one of these available for every child participating in the activity.
2. Allow the children to each pick at least one positive affirmation from the list or create one of their own.
3. Have them write (if they are able) their affirmation somewhere on the anchor page. Help those who need it by writing their sentence for them.
4. Have the participants decorate their page with a pencil, markers, crayons, or whatever is available.

EMOTIONAL AWARENESS

5. (Optional) Laminate their image with transparent packing tape (if it's on a notecard) or a page protector (if on paper) so that their creation is durable.
6. Allow the children to keep this image with them, to remind them that the storm will always pass and that their affirmation will always be accurate even in the darkest of days.

List of Affirmations:

1. I am creative, and I have a fantastic imagination.
2. I am intelligent, and my future is so bright.
3. I have so many unique skills and talents!
4. Math is super easy for me. I am destined for great things.
5. My friends and family love me.
6. I am so compassionate and kind to those around me.
7. My confidence expands when I seek out new experiences.
8. I am so loyal to the people I love.
9. I will always stand up for those who can't stand up for themselves.
10. I am not afraid to do the right thing.
11. Whatever happens, I will make it through.
12. My mistakes are making me better.
13. The storm will always pass, and things will always get better.
14. No one can hold me back from who I am meant to be.
15. Every single day is a new chance to be great.

16. I am always learning and growing my knowledge.

17. Failures are a necessary part of the growing process.

18. I love and believe in myself.

19. Today, I am going to live my life with courage.

20. I will always pick myself back up.

Chapter 3
Anti-anxiety

CHAPTER 3
ANTI-ANXIETY

Stress is a genuine threat to today's youth, as it seems to mount more and more with every passing generation. Through these exercises, you can help the children in your life learn to cope with their tension. Meditations, contemplations, games, and activities offer little ones the opportunity to analyze their own conquer their doubt.

10) PEACEFUL BREATHING

This exercise could also be referred to as Breath Control, but that moniker is not nearly as interesting to children. By taking charge of the air we inhale and then exhale, we can signal to the brain that everything is alright. Sometimes a maladjusted *fight or flight* response causes our mind to send stress hormones throughout our body when there is nothing to fear.

Breathing exercises may efficiently be utilized anytime the child needs to calm themselves down. These activities are short and straightforward, allowing for memorization. Pick out a stimulating day to begin practicing the following.

11) EASY COUNTING

Our ancestors lived in a very hectic world full of risk and danger. The brains of our forefathers were wired to always watch for trouble. The same signals in your mind that cause inconvenient worry or anxiety were their lifelines, saving them from scary saber-toothed tigers.

For this exercise, we are going to practice taking super deep breaths. First, inhale through your nose and pull the air all the way down into your stomach (hold for a count of three). Exhale in a slow and steady stream, from your mouth.

Place one of your hands upon your stomach and watch as it rises and falls with the breaths you take. Remember, if you are ever doing this on your own, pull the air all the way down into your belly, holding it there for three seconds. Part of controlling your breathing involves counting.

We are going to take some super deep breaths together now, as we count to ten.

Breathe in, one.

Breathe out, two.

Breathe in, three.

Breathe out, four.

Breathe in, five.

Breathe out, six.

Breathe in, seven.

Breathe out, eight.

Breathe in, nine.

Breathe out, ten.

The next time you feel fear when there isn't anything around to cause the feeling, try breathing and counting. Know that your emotions are entirely normal. You may calm yourself by slowing down for a moment and practicing this exercise.

12) A BEAUTIFUL FLOWER

Imagine that you are holding the most extraordinary flower in the world. The petals are covered in your favorite colors and so many unusual shapes and swirls. You have never seen such a fantastic bloom.

Place your flower in front of your nose, and slowly inhale air as though you are trying to smell your bloom. You want to savor the experience, so you are breathing in through a slow and steady stream. Hold that air in your chest, as though you can absorb the scent inside your body. When you are ready to exhale, do so gently through your mouth.

Repeat these this breathing pattern four times.

13) RABBIT NOSED

Close your eyes and imagine that you are an adorable little rabbit with caramel-colored fur and a tiny pink nose. To become the bunny, you must breathe like the bunny. Sniff the air in three shorts bursts, wiggling your nose as you go.

Exhale in one long stream of air through your nose. Repeat this action while making your breath-out a little longer and slower with each cycle. Continue with your rabbit breaths for just a few more moments.

14) A SNAKE'S HISS

Breathe in through your nose, in a long and steady stream. Pull the air deep down, all the way to your stomach, and hold it there for a count of three. Exhale slowly through your mouth, making a low hissing sound (like a snake) as the air exits your body.

15) 3-4-3

- Inhale through your nose as you count to three in your head.
- Pull your breath down into your chest and stomach. Feel that region of your body expanding.
- Hold your air in your chest and belly as you count to four in your head.
- Exhale through your mouth as you count to three.
- If you feel uncomfortable, change your counts to two f0r the inhale, three for holding, and then two again for the exhale.
- Repeat this cycle five times.

16) WAVE BREATHING

- Close your eyes and imagine that you are standing on a beach, watching the waves crashing against the shore.
- You can smell the saltwater and feel the breeze against your face.
- Breathe in and out as though your breath is the water in the sea, coming into the shore and then leaving again.
- With each wave, the water recedes a little further out. Slowly lengthen your breaths in and out, in time with the waves.
- Your inhalations and exhales should be slow and rhythmic, as your body gently sways back and forth.
- Continue breathing in this way for a few more moments.

17) HAND BREATHING

Hold one hand out in front of you with your fingers spread apart and with your other hand, form a pointing gesture. Place the tip of your extended finger at the bottom joint of your other thumb. Now, take a deep breath to get ready for this small exercise.

You are going to trace along the outside of your spread hand with slow and steady motion. As you go up the side of a finger, you are going to breathe in. When you go down the side of a finger, breathe out.

Try breathing as you trace the outline of your open palm. Inhale as you climb and exhale as you fall. When you have finished tracing your hand (ending with the pinkie finger), you have completed the exercise.

ANTI-ANXIETY

18) QUICK EXERCISES

The following methods may be used when children are worried. Teach participating kids these techniques so that they are better able to self-soothe in stressful situations. Carrying these small tricks around will help to change the way strong emotions are handled at the moment.

19) EMBRACE YOURSELF

There are parts of our brain that naturally react when we are comforted through touch. The next time you feel overwhelmed, try being a calming presence for yourself. Hug yourself for a little instant relief from big feelings.

Self-hugging may even be accomplished without anyone else knowing! Try crossing your arms close to your body and giving yourself a warm embrace. Your arms may fold over your stomach, as your hands rest on your sides.

20) EARMUFFS

Ancient medicine has always explored the role ears play in soothing us. It may sound silly, but the next time you find yourself in a bad mood, try gently pinching the outside of your ear. Work your way from the top, all the way down to the earlobe.

To start this method, make a pincer with your hand by extending your thumb and the finger you use to point. You want your hand to resemble a crab's claw, try opening and closing your pincher a few times. We are not applying too much pressure to our ears, just a little.

Start at the top of the ear and pinch with your claw for three seconds. Move down along the outline, holding for the same amount of time at every new place. When you have finally pressed on your earlobe, you may stop.

21) HOLDING A HAND

Did you know that holding someone's hand as been scientifically proven to help with feelings of worry and anxiety? Next time you are worried, and there are no free hands, try holding your own. Lace your fingers together and hang on until you begin to feel better.

22) GRATEFUL HAND

For a couple of minutes every single day, stop and take a moment to appreciate the gifts that you have been given. Hold up an open hand in front of you and think of reasons that you can be thankful. Count your blessings to yourself, putting down a finger for every reason. Each day, you should have five new reasons to appreciate the world around you and the people in your life.

23) GROUNDING STONE

In this exercise, we are going to be making another object that the child may carry around as a reminder that stressful situations will always end. Decorating the stones allows a relaxing craft day between guardian and little one. Whenever they are feeling stressed, they may pull out their small rock.

ANTI-ANXIETY

Running fingers along the surface should help children stay grounded in the present moment. They may also associate their stone with their favorite positive affirmation, using the object to remind them of something pleasant. The stone is also an enduring force and a reminder that all stresses are temporary.

MATERIALS NEEDED:

Smooth river stone

Pencil

Acrylic paint

INSTRUCTIONS:

1. Help the participating children design and paint a river stone that they may carry around with them.
2. Outline the designs in pencil.
3. Use acrylic paint to complete the artwork on the stones and then allow it to dry.

24) STRESS BALL

This is one of the most beloved and well-known activities related to relieving stress, but it is famous for a reason. Stress balls are easy to make, fun to play with, and they work well when it comes to taking an anxious squeeze or two. The exercise is going to be an easy and inexpensive way to put a smile on a child's face.

MATERIALS NEEDED:

- Balloons (multiple).
- Rice, flour, or dry beans.
- Plastic funnel.
- Child-safe scissors.
- Markers (Optional).

INSTRUCTIONS:

1. Pick the filling that you intend to use for participating children.
2. Double the balloons by sliding one inside of another, and then straightening them up. Reinforcing the material will protect the object from bursting or causing a mess.
3. Put the tube end of the funnel through the opening for the balloons and begin to add the filling.
4. Tie the balloons when enough material has been added to them and then cut away the additional rubber.
5. Enjoy!

25) A SUNNY MEDITATION

The following meditation is aimed at relaxing and unwinding during stimulating days. A Sunny Meditation can be practiced at any point in the day, whenever a little peace and stillness are needed. Make sure that all participating children have shaken the extra energy from their

ANTI-ANXIETY

limbs before beginning so that everyone is willing and able to keep still for just a few moments.

Find a quiet room with little distraction. Instruct the participating kids to sit with their legs crossed and their hands facing palm-up in their lap. Remind every to ensure that they are not too hunched over, so the activity is comfortable.

THE SCRIPT:

I would like for all of you to close your eyes and think about all the different sorts of deep breaths we have practiced so far. So many of these breathing exercises require you to inhale and hold air deep inside your stomach, instead of just your chest. Concentrate on the sound of my voice and the sound of the air cycling through your body.

Place one hand on top of your stomach, for just a few minutes. Pay attention to the way your belly rises and falls as you breathe. We are going to take a few deep breaths, inhaling all the way down.

Count to ten as you breathe. One for your inhale, two for your exhale. Three for your inhale, four for your exhale. Five for your inhale, six for your exhale. Seven for your inhale, eight for your exhale. Nine for your inhale, and finally, ten as you exhale.

You may now allow your hand to fall back into your lap, and you can go back to breathing in your regular pattern. Take a moment to relax into this position. Keep listening to my voice and the sounds of your body.

Imagine that you are standing in a beautiful green field. Above you, the weather is nice and sunny. The sky is most a clear blue, except for a few fluffy white clouds.

You hear a mysterious whooshing sound behind you. You turn around slowly to see one of those puffy clouds waiting on the ground; it is waiting for you. Gradually, you walk over to the wispy white cushion.

You sit down on the edge of the cloud suspended in front of you, allowing your feet to dangle over the edge as it begins to lift off of the ground. The world around you is peaceful and safe. There are no other creatures, except for you and your new cloud friend.

Falling back into the cloud feels like landing on a luxurious mattress made of vapor and the softest features. The white whisps engulf you, cooling your skin. With every single breath you take, you sink further into the drifting cloud.

You are traveling over fields of splendid flowers of all shapes and colors. The air is perfumed with the sweetness of candy and roses. Your cloud is dutifully carrying you along through this beautiful wonderland.

Up ahead, you see the most glorious mountain range, bathed in the soft light of the midday sun. There are a few more clouds in the distance; some of these are a light gray color. You can almost see the hazy sheets of rain falling from the heavens. Continue listening to the sound of your own breathing.

As you continue forward, you can see the rains quickly disappearing. The storm fades as though it is honoring your presence. Suddenly, there is a brilliant rainbow in its place. The colors are so vivid and intense; the rainbow seems to glow.

Your cloud is moving closer and closer to the rainbow, and it becomes apparent that you are going to pass through it. You are

ANTI-ANXIETY

becoming more and more relaxed. The glowing colors are waiting for you just ahead.

As you make your way through the rainbow, you can feel the colors touching your skin. The glow feels warm and fuzzy like you are being engulfed by your favorite blanket. Every muscle the rainbow touches begins to release its tension. You feel the stress and tightness leaving your body as you are refreshed by the light.

When you have passed entirely through the brilliant glowing rainbow, your cloud gently places you down on the top of a splendid mountain. You can see the entire valley in front of you. Take in a few deep breaths before you open your eyes once more and rejoin the waking world.

26) LEARNING TO FOCUS FOR MEDITATION

This lesson is all about relaxing tension and easing anxiety through a release of energy from the body. We all carry our stress in different places, and learning to target particular muscle groups for the release of tension can be beneficial. Many of the meditations that we will use going forward utilize this technique.

THE SCRIPT:

The human body is a miraculous thing! Today we are going to learn how to tune into our bodies to better help with relaxation. Focusing your attention is an important trick to know for future meditations.

I want you to bring your attention to your fingers, as though you are going to move them. Instead of wiggling your fingers, you are going to relax them in the same way you relax your face after a big smile. Just allow your muscles to be ultimately at rest.

Now, try focusing on your shoulder. Bringing your attention to the muscle should allow you to feel how much tension it is holding. Allow your shoulders to relax completely; there should be no movement.

Sometimes we clench muscles without even noticing. Bring your attention to your eyebrows and forehead. I bet that those muscles were tense; release them just as you would a smile.

Practice this new power, as it can be used to relax you completely! Focusing your attention and releasing the tension is actually going to be featured so many of our new meditations. Try loosening the muscles in your neck, stomach, chest, legs, and all over.

If you ever get confused about releasing the tension, smile, and then relax your face. Every muscle group can be controlled in the same way. In A Quick Meditation for Relaxation, we will use this technique.

27) A QUICK MEDITATION FOR RELAXATION

This exercise is perfect for those times the children in your life need an instant dose of relaxation and release. Stress and tension are no match for this classic meditation, designed to bring peace and comfort to any day. Children often become fidgety during long periods of stillness, so try this activity for a fast cure for stress.

Instruct participating children to sit with their legs crossed and their hands resting comfortably in their lap.

ANTI-ANXIETY

THE SCRIPT:

Practice bringing your awareness to your feet. Feel all of the sensations that your toes are experiencing at this moment. Now try moving your attention to your hands, as though you are going to move them but without actually doing so.

During this exercise, you are going to focus on different parts of your body. You will bring your attention to the sensations surrounding that limb or muscle group without moving. You have the ability to shift your awareness to any part of you; we are going to explore this ability through this relaxing meditation.

Close your eyes and listen only to the sound of my voice and your own breathing. If your thoughts threaten to carry you away, simply redirect your attention back to the rhythmic airflow. Wandering minds are natural, but inner words will eventually quiet down.

We are going to take a few deep breaths, slowly. Breathe in and hold your air inside while you count to three inside your head, and then breathe out again. Inhale and hold it, then exhale.

Bring the air all the way down into your stomach as you inhale, hold, and then exhale again. Breathe in, hold the air, and exhale. Breathe in, hold the air, and exhale. You may now relax and return to your regular pattern.

There is a ball of blue light in the sky; it is glowing and crackling above you. The orb begins to come to you. Feel the wind from the moving object against your face as it approaches. The item stops in front of you, remaining suspended in the air.

The light enters your body at your feet, through your muscles. Every muscle that is touched by the warm fizzy energy is relaxed. Your limbs are getting heavier and heavier as the tension leaves your body.

Bring your awareness to the muscles in your calves, feel the tension leaving as the light rises through your body. Move your attention to your thighs and feel the stress melting away in the glow. With every breath, you are sinking lower and lower.

Feel your stomach relaxing as you are bathed in the glow of the blue energy. The light is slowly moving up through your torso and into your chest. Tension and stress in your muscles disappear.

Focus on your arms and shoulders now, as the light moves through those muscles. Your neck is relaxed by the glow. When the energy moves into your face, feel your jaw unclench, and your brow unfurrow.

The beautiful blue light leaves your body through your head. You feel completely relaxed and refreshed. Take a few moments to sit in silence before you proceed with your day, a new person.

28) GLITTER JAR STRESS TOOL

In this exercise, the children are going to create an object similar to a snow globe but with colorful glitter. They should be encouraged to see the sparkles symbolically, attaching it to their emotion. Participating children may even select their colors based upon associations they have made with feelings.

ANTI-ANXIETY

MATERIALS NEEDED:

- Mason Jar with Lid
- Glitter
- Water
- Craft Glue
- Paper Towel
- Superglue (optional)
- Food Coloring (optional)
- Permanent Marker (optional)

INSTRUCTIONS:

1. Fill a mason jar three/fourths full of water.
2. Add in a generous squeeze of glue.
3. Drop-in a few drops of your food coloring and lots of glitters
4. Ensure that the rim of the jar is dry with the paper towel, before adding a little superglue and twisting the lid on (**tight**). Ensure that you are the only one to touch the superglue.
5. Older children may decorate the outside of their jar with a permanent marker if desired.

Encourage the children to shake their jar when the glue has dried. Instruct the participating kids to watch their container as all the chaos inside finally settles down at the bottom. They should feel a sense of calm as order returns to the jar.

29) RELAXATION STRETCHING

Sometimes anxiety can manifest a physical tenseness in the body. Relieving some of that tension can help to lift moods and ease minds. Relax a little with the following exercises, as we endeavor to shake off extra tightness. Have participating children stand with their arms by their sides, to begin.

30) CAT SCRATCH STRETCHING

THE SCRIPT:

Imagine that you are a sleepy cat who has just woken up from a nap. Stretch your arms all the way out in front of you, interlocking your fingers with your palms facing away from you. What sensations do you feel in your arms and hands? Does it feel as though your muscles are waking up from a nap? Let out one loud "MEOW" before we continue.

Raise your interlocked paws slowly over your head, while keeping your arms straight. Go as far back as you are able and feel the relaxing pull of your muscles as they release stored tension. Bring your arms back down again until your hands are back in front of you. Now relax your arms.

You are now going to make a fist with your paws, and you are going to squeeze your hands together (like you are squishing a stress ball) while you count to five before relaxing again. After you have finished with this stretch, hold your hands up with your palms facing away from you. Bend your thumb down across your palm. Fold all o your other fingers down at the knuckle.

It should seem as though you have a cat paw, with your thumb being the only finger touching your palm. Hold this gesture for a count of ten. You may now relax your hands and allow them to rest by your side. Do your fingers feel better after the stretching exercise?

31) DOWNWARD DOG

Our next stretch is actually a reasonably infamous yoga pose. Don't attempt this stretch unless the floor is clean, or the participants have access to a mat. Downward Dog is a simple position meant to relieve tension in the legs.

THE SCRIPT:

Get down on your hands and knees, as if you are pretending to be a dog. Slowly straighten your legs as you switch your weight from your knees to your feet. Your center of balance will feel as though it is moving backward. When you have finished, you will look like an upside-down letter 'V' with your bottom being the highest joint of the letter.

Hold this pose for fifteen seconds, or as long as you are able. When you have finished, your legs should feel outstanding. All your muscles will be stretched out and renewed.

32) BACK AND LEG STRETCH

This next stretch starts from a cross-legged position on the floor. The pose would be helpful for waking the body up after meditation. The muscle groups targeted in this exercise are those of the back, hips, and sides.

THE SCRIPT:

Sit on the floor with your legs crossed in front of you. Lean forward as though you have just fainted! You may cross your arms in front of you so that your forehead is resting on your forearms.

Feel the muscles in your back and sides being pulled as you stretch. Hold this pose for fifteen seconds before sitting up and relaxing. Shake your arms and hands to release any left-over tension.

You may then straighten your legs out in front of you, with your heel resting on the floor. Reach for the tips of your toes for a count of five before relaxing again. Do not worry if you aren't able to touch your toes; this exercise is about stretching and not flexibility.

Chapter 4
Concentration

CHAPTER 4

CONCENTRATION

The exercises in this chapter will deal with focus and concentration. Each the activities will center around helping kids fine-tune their ability to pay attention. Through fun challenges, participants will grow better at understanding their own minds and their unique learning styles.

33) THE BELL

This exercise is called the bell, but it could be done with any short sound. You will need to ask all participating children to take a seat. Ring the bell (or play another related sound) once for them. Ask the children (or child) what they noticed about the sound.

You will then instruct the participants to close their eyes and relax. Direct them to listen to the sound very closely, this time. Inform your audience that they will be asked if they can pinpoint when the sound stopped. Play the sound again and pose the following questions.

1. Did the noise end abruptly, or did it fade away?

2. Could you pinpoint the moment the sound ended?

CONCENTRATION

3. How was the experience different when your eyes were shut?
4. Did you notice anything about the noise that you missed the first time?
5. Did you see a shape or color when the sound played the second time?

34) THE PINPOINT

One of the most critical pieces of learning mindfulness is the ability to manage our thoughts and feelings. We can only take in a finite amount of information, and sometimes, our thoughts are clouded by other things. Teaching children to focus on one singular object will afford them the chance to control their attention. Concentration can be taught through practice.

The following exercise is meant to teach kids to focus on their surroundings. Even as adults, it can be so easy to miss essential details due to the speed at which our mind seems to operate. Intrusive thoughts only add to the difficulty of offering one subject or object undivided attention.

THE SCRIPT:

I want you to look around the room and pick out one particular thing to observe. Note the size, shape, and color of the object you select. Concentrate on your subject for ten full seconds.

In the beginning, you will likely find thoughts bursting through your attempts to observe your surroundings. Do not fight these stray thoughts or feelings. Your only job is to redirect your attention back to the object that you were studying.

Try picking about six different objects, noticing as many details as you are able to take in. Try not to look at more than one thing at a time; keep your sight limited to your subject. Move your gaze around the room with intention and purpose.

The point of this exercise is to learn to manage the intrusive thoughts, instead of fighting against them. Remember to acknowledge wandering thoughts and then return to the subject you are watching. Do not fight the words or images that fly into your head.

35) MYSTERY BAG

In this exercise, children are required to lean on their sense of touch to discern different objects without the benefit of sight. The Mystery Bag activity requires participants to reach into a bag that is filled with objects curated by you. By picking everyday items with strange shapes, you require the kids the use their concentration and memory to decide that they are feeling.

When putting together your bag, it can be fun to consider shape, texture, and temperature. A stone or coin might feel cold compared to a rubber object. Try not to pick obscure items, but also avoid making the selections too easy to guess.

You may help the participants along by giving them hints or making suggestions, but you should refrain from giving them the answer. The Mystery Bag activity should ignite their imagination and maybe even

CONCENTRATION

provide a few laughs. As they are feeling the objects, ask that they describe surfaces, temperatures, edges, and textures.

MATERIALS NEEDED:

- An opaque bag that cannot be seen through.
- A random assortment of objects from around the house or classroom.

THE SCRIPT:

We are going to try a new exercise where individually; you reach inside a bag and feel for one item. Once you have selected your object, use your sense of touch to decide that you believe you're holding. Through this activity, you are going to notice details that you may have never picked up on before!

You must keep your eyes closed when standing beside the bag. Should you need to open your eyes for a moment, you must turn your head. As you are feeling the object, describe the experience aloud. Touch a particular item until you are ready to guess what you are holding.

1. Were you able to correctly guess your item?
2. Were there any corners, textures, or edges that you had never noticed on the object before now?
3. Did you find this exercise to be exciting or frustrating?
4. Do you enjoy discovering new things?

36) LEAVES AND DETAILS

Leaves and Details is an intricate exercise that accomplishes many objectives related to mindfulness and takes up at least an hour or two. You and the children participating in the activity are going to take a walk outside in a forest (or wooded area). If you are unable to enter into the woods for this activity, then you may skip the first few steps.

As you and the participating children are walking through the trees, have them concentrate on the world around them. The forest is full of life that we might miss if we are talking or daydreaming about other things. Ask the kids to pay attention to the beautiful colors of the leaves, dirt, trees, and stones. Sounds, smells, and the environment should also be observed on the stroll.

As you are walking along, have each child pick up three leaves. The spare foliage will be used in a project once you have all returned to your shelter. Interesting pebbles may be taken too, as long as no one brings back anything living or valuable.

When you have returned to your home or the classroom, have a discussion about the forest and all of the fantastic things that everyone noticed. Sharing experiences with the class may provide details from some children that others may have missed. Ask about colors, textures, sounds, smells, and feelings.

PART TWO:

Alternative: If you were not able to take a walk in the forest, then stop on your own time and gather a few leaves. You may also just go

CONCENTRATION

to the supermarket and pick a flower or small bouquet. The children will be concentrating on these items for part two of the exercise; As long as you bring flora, the activity will work great. Flowers may even provoke some more colorful responses.

For part two of this exercise, you are going to have the children do a short breathing exercise with their eyes closed. Taking a few deep breaths is also acceptable; we just want to reset their eyes so they will be better able to appreciate the leaves. The participants will then concentrate on the flora before them.

They will be asked to notice the way the veins run through the leaves. The colors (especially during the autumn months), the smells, and the way the vegetation feels in their hands. This activity serves to teach children to observe with more than just their eyes by using all of their senses to engage with their surroundings.

INSTRUCTIONS:

1. Gather the children and take a walk in the forest, during which they should be instructed to pay close attention to their environment.
    a. Concentrate on sight, smell, touch, and sound.
2. Ask the children to pick a few leaves during the stroll.
3. When you return back to your home/classroom, the children will take a brief break by closing their eyes and breathing deeply; this will promote calm and enable them to notice details in their leaves (or flower).

4. The leaves (or flower) will be observed for details, requiring the children to concentrate on the objects in front of them.

37) DRAWING YOUR BREATH

This exercise is a really unique and exciting activity that requires both focus and abstract thinking. Sometimes we must turn the concentration inward, as mindfulness is as much about knowing oneself as it is about self-acceptance. Drawing your breath is an easy and therapeutic way to give yourself some much-needed attention.

MATERIALS NEEDED:

- Paper
- Pencil, crayons, colored pencils, or markers

INSTRUCTIONS:

1. Have the children close their eyes and breathe deeply for a few cycles.

    a. You may use one of the breathing exercises from chapter three, or you can just guide them through taking a few deep breaths.

2. Ask the participating children to visualize their breath as a line in their mind, as they are inhaling and exhaling. Then ask them to draw the picture they saw, transferring it from their own imaginations to the empty page.

CONCENTRATION

    a. The image is likely to be abstract and will be different for every child.

    b. They do not have to overthink this exercise; they are only drawing a representation of what they saw in their mind. It might be a line that rises when the participants inhale and falls when they exhale, or it might be a strange line that turns in upon itself jumbles up before straightening out again. There is no wrong answer.

3. Direct the children to play around with their breathing (in a safe way) to see how it changes their line. See what happens when the breath is shallower or when they take lots of small breaths.

Hopefully, this exercise will inspire the children (or child) that you are working with to become creative. They may want to explain their drawing, or they could use the illustration as a base for another sketch. Making artwork with your breathing could be a fun way to start or end the day.

38) A CONCENTRATION GAME

This exercise will allow for a more fun way to understand the power of concentration and observation when they work together. Play this game when you are working with more than one child for the best results. Memory and the ability to absorb and describe details will come in handy!

MATERIALS NEEDED:

- Notecards
- Small pictures, from magazines or books, of everyday items.
- Glue
- Pencils

INSTRUCTIONS

1. Cut out kid-friendly images from magazines and books, of items that the children might see often. Example:
    a. Tables with chairs.
    b. Animals.
    c. Nail polish.
    d. Cell phone
    e. Door
2. Glue each image to a notecard and write the simple form of the word beneath the photo.
    a. A picture of a vehicle should be labeled "car" and not "Brand 'X' 2001 XL 4WD".
3. Shuffle the cards around and allow each child to pull one. Allow a few minutes for undisturbed observation and concentration.
4. Each child will then have a turn to describe their image to the class without using the word written on their notecard or any brand names.

CONCENTRATION

5. The person who guesses their classmate's image correctly wins a point.

39) SCREEN MEDITATION

The following meditation can be used to inspire creativity and encourage focus for children. The short exercise can be performed whenever the day needs a little color. Instruct the participating children to sit with their legs crossed. Kids may also choose to lay down with their hands at their sides if the floor is clean or mats are available.

THE SCRIPT:

I would like for you to close your eyes and take a few deep breaths with me. We are going to pull the air all the way into our stomachs as we inhale, holding it there while we count to three quietly. Listen to the sound of my voice and the noise the air makes as it travels through our throat and into your lungs.

Let us count as we breathe. One for the inhale and two for the exhale. Three as we breathe in again, and four as we breathe out. Five in and six out. Seven on the inhale and then eight on the exhale. Breathe-in to nine and breathe out to ten.

Now I would like you to imagine that you are sitting in a completely black room. Should you have any intrusive thoughts, accept them, and then return your attention to the darkened room. It is absolutely normal to become distracted, simply acknowledge, and rejoin.

The black room feels like nighttime, and it is entirely safe. There is nothing that can get you as you stand at the edge of the darkened room. Listen to the sound of my voice as your limbs are becoming heavier and heavier.

Wait, there is something in front of you. A large white square has just emerged from the darkness. It seems as though a screen has just turned on, directing before you. You watch as an image begins to appear through the haze.

What is appearing on your screen? What sounds do you hear coming from the images? Is it a film or a picture? What colors, so you see in your own unique vision?

Take a moment to observe the display in front of you. What do these images make you feel? Can you smell anything coming from the screen? Concentrate on your screen and absorb all of the details that lay before you.

You may now open your eyes. What do you think your imagination was trying to tell you? Take a moment to think about your answer before we continue with the day.

Note: To extend this activity, you may also have the children draw a representation of the images that played on their screen.

40) THE AMAZING APPLE

The Amazing Apple is another exercise that allows children to use their skills with concentration as well as their imagination. All of our senses are connected to our memories. Using a piece of fruit that

CONCENTRATION

every child is familiar with will allow them to call upon details that they have observed in the past.

MATERIALS NEEDED:

- An apple.
- You may need more than one, depending on how many children are participating in this activity.

THE SCRIPT:

Take a look at the apple sitting in front of you. I know that all of you have had apples before, so this exercise should be easy. I want you to think back in your memories!

Recall the way the apple skin feels beneath your fingers. Is the fruit smooth? Is it rough? Does the skin have a rubbery texture?

Remember the way the apple smelled. Does it have a sour scent, or is it sweet? How does the aroma change once the fruit has been peeled?

Close your eyes and think about the way the apple tastes and the texture of the fruit's flesh. Was the inside sweet? Was it warm? Are apples juicy or dry inside?

Keep your eyes closed and visualize the apple in front of you. Can you recall how it looks without opening your eyes?

From now on, when you observe different objects, I want you to involve all of your senses. When you find yourself thinking of an apple, imagine the way that it feels and how the pale inside tastes. Feel the slight chill on your tongue and the strange texture of the flesh. Imagine the way it feels inside your hands or the smell that always hangs in the air around the fruit.

41) DISTRACTION

This exercise will highlight the brain's multitasking abilities (or lack thereof) with the use of a typical stacking game like Jenga. Children will have a chance to play the game twice, allowing them the opportunity to observe the way their undivided attention can change the quality of the outcome. Kids will love this activity, and it is sure to bring about a few laughs.

MATERIALS NEEDED:

- Jenga or a similar game
- A device that can play music

INSTRUCTIONS:

1. Instruct the participating children to play a game of Jenga while there is music playing in the background.
    a. If you are playing the game with only one kid, then engage the child in conversation. You could play the television in the background instead of music. Do whatever you can to make the environment busy, so concentration is split between the room and the game.

CONCENTRATION

    b. If you are playing the game with multiple children, then encourage them all to chat with each other.

2. When the first round is completed, play the same game again with a quiet environment. Allow the children to focus on their gameplay and see how much longer the tower lasts.

This project will demonstrate the difference between focusing on activities and splitting your attention. Projects, work, and even games are more successful when they have an individual's undivided attention. The brain cannot concentrate on multiple things at once, without sacrificing accuracy.

Chapter 5
Observation

CHAPTER 5
OBSERVATION

The exercises in this chapter will encourage improvement in children's observational skills. Fun games and activities challenge little ones to pay attention to their surroundings. Awareness is a useful skill, both inside and outside of the self.

Children will learn to notice details that they may have never seen before inside everyday scenes. You will guide your participants on a journey to discover the world around them, down to the smallest details. Kids learn best through exploration, and you will be their guide.

42) SUPER SENSES

This exercise will be simple and a lot of fun for all those involved. Use the following only if you can leave the house (or classroom) for a walk. You do not have to go outside but just aim for an area that you are not often occupying. The forest is preferred for all of the varying types of textures, shapes, smells, and colors, but anywhere new will work.

Superheroes and Sherlock Holmes have something in common; they can use their senses for observation. You will direct your participants to walk around a new area for a few minutes. When you return to your home/classroom, you will ask them questions about their experience. Hopefully, they noticed some interesting details!

INSTRUCTIONS:

1. Explain to the participating children that they will be turning their senses up for the following activity. They are going to pay close attention to their surroundings to see if they notice anything new.

2. The exercise will begin with a walk around a familiar space (wherever you and the children spend most of your time together). Walk the group around the room before exiting for a walk outside (or in a new place).

3. Explore the new area with your group. Ensure that they are concentrating on their senses and on getting to know their environment.

4. When you return to the home/class, ask them questions regarding what they have discovered.

    a. Did you notice anything new in our familiar environment?

    b. What did you see along the walk?

    c. Did you hear anything as we were walking?

    d. Were there any smells that stood out to you?

    e. Did you touch anything along the walk?

OBSERVATION

43) BONUS ROUND!

If you were able to take a walk through the woods during the summer months, have the children search trees for the exoskeletons of cicadas that have been left on tree trunks. Explain that the cicadas are still living (probably in the trees making lots of noise), but they must shed their old skin to develop their wings.

Searching for cicada's exoskeletons is a wonderful way to test out observational powers because they are such exciting specimens. The shells blend into the tree bark, making them difficult to spot with the naked eye, but they are also large. The empty husks will be about the size of a child's thumb. The insect's metamorphosis can also provide an excellent transition into a conversation about bugs and the natural world.

Most species of cicada live as nymphs far below the topsoil for around seventeen years before they finally crawl up to leave their shell on a nearby tree trunk. That means that the exoskeleton will likely be older than everyone else on the nature walk (outside of yourself). If those participating in the exercise happen upon the empty shell, tell them to listen to the sounds coming from the tops of the trees. They are likely to hear the insect's powerful song echoing out.

44) WHAT IS THE POINT OF THIS?

This book has placed a lot of emphasis on being able to use the senses to observe the world around us. There is a reason that concentration, focus, and observation are so extraordinarily important. Being able to give a project, subject, job, or person your full attention will improve your general success, but there is something more nuanced hidden within these exercises.

Mindfulness means that an individual is present in the moment while accepting their thoughts and feelings. Observation can act as a tether to the moment of which we are speaking. When someone is giving the entirety of their attention to the task at hand, their thoughts aren't somewhere else. The mind may wander, but it is always directed back to now.

Most of our worry and stress come from dwelling on thoughts that have no influence on our present experience. Kicking those feelings out to concentrate on what is happening now can do incredible amounts of good for mental health. Building these habits in children means that they are not going to be burdened with the same issues that many of their peers face.

We want children to be able to manage their emotions while remaining engaged with the present. Kids can concentrate and observe with their senses to ground themselves to the current moment. Being asked to find a cicada's exoskeleton is just the most entertaining way to achieve the desired outcome.

45) THREE CHANGES

We have all seen those ads for games online that ask you how many changes between two identical pictures you can spot. This is a physical game inspired by the virtual classic. This activity is likely to be a hit at home or in the classroom.

OBSERVATION

You are going to arrange the kids into two lines, facing each other. If you are doing these activities with one child, then you will stand opposite of your participant. You will also be required to play the game if you are working with an odd number of children.

You may need props for this game (though it could be played without). Place a small container filled with props on either side of the line and keep it covered until the children are ready to use them. At no point should the other row of children be able to see the opposite side's accessories.

MATERIALS NEEDED:

- Props that you can wear.
- These should be small/subtle items.
- You can use a pencil behind the ear or a sticker on your hand. You don't have to buy props if you would rather not, just have small items on-hand.

INSTRUCTIONS:

1. The children will be playing in pairs. The two participants facing one another are involved in a game.
2. The children are going to take a full minute to observe one another before the round starts.
3. Announce that it is time to "turn around." The children will turn, with their backs facing one another.

4. As they are turned away from each other, each child will change three things about themselves. They can use the secret props that have been made available to each side.

5. When the time comes to turn back around, the children will have another minute to observe the person standing opposite of them.

6. Each child must guess what three things the person across from them has changed.

    a. They could have placed a pen in their pocket.

    b. The opposite child could be wearing a new necklace.

    c. The other player might have changed something about their hair.

7. When the round has been completed, and everyone has guessed, one line of children will rotate, shifting their positions in one direction or another so that each child has a new opponent.

46) MATCHING GAME

This is another variation of a beloved classic game. Children will enjoy both the craft and the game aspect of this exercise, which will help enhance their observational prowess. If you are performing these activities with one child, then you will be involved with the deck-making process.

Do you remember playing the matching game as a child? Lots of cards were laid out in front of you facedown. There were always two

OBSERVATION

of each image. You selected two cards to flip, at a time, to try and achieve as many pairs as possible.

You and the children participating in the activity are going to be making your own set of matching cards. This activity will allow the little ones to use their crafting skills to create something that they can actually use. Observational skills will also be put to the test during the game.

MATERIALS NEEDED:

- Notecards of one color
- Pencils
- Markers, crayons, or colored pencils
- Rubber bands
- Sealable plastic bag or freezer bag

INSTRUCTIONS:

1. The children will need to create at least ten pairs of cards. Each child should be responsible for at least one pair.
    a. You can have as many cards as you have participants.
    b. If you are working with one child, you may each make five pairs (ten cards in total).
2. Lay the cards out (facedown) in rows of five.
3. Each child will take turns, turning over two cards.

    a. If you are working with one child, you and the little one may alternate turns.
4. The player who has the most matches at the end of the game wins.
5. Wrap a rubber band around your new deck and then place it inside a sealable plastic bag.

47) LONG TERM OBSERVATION

Long-Term observation is such a rewarding activity, with a few caveats. This exercise works best when you have access to a park (preferably a wooded park), a garden, or a forest. If your group is large enough, you may need more chaperons for this outing.

Observational skills must be practiced, and doing so over a long period of time can be especially helpful. Use the changing seasons as a way to occupy the minds of children. They will learn to be still and to take in the information around them, even if the art takes a little time.

MATERIALS NEEDED:

- A park or other safe, natural area
- If you have a large group, then you may need additional supervision as the children are going to be spread out.
- You will need to have access to this place regularly, to instill the habit in the participating children.
- Journals and writing utensils are helpful for older children.

OBSERVATION

INSTRUCTIONS:

1. Ask each child to find a comfortable and private space to sit (where they are safe, and you are still able to monitor them). They will need to avoid picking a spot too close to others; engaging in conversation will be tempting.

2. The children will observe changes to their surrounding every single visit—plan to visit the park/forest at least two times per season, preferably twice a month.

3. The older children will record the changes they witness in the park.
    a. Has the weather changed?
    b. Do the leaves and plants look different?
    c. Is the temperature different?
    d. How does the area smell?
    e. Is it more or less populated now?
    f. What animals do you see?
    g. Are there any birds chirping?
    h. How do the shadows look each time?
    i. What sorts of flowers are blooming?

The children should feel free to add information of their own as the project progresses. This is one of the few long-term exercises within this book. I hope that you and your group can make time for the visits.

48) SCAVENGER HUNT

Scavenger Hunt is an easily customizable activity that allows you to scale up or scale down the amount of effort that goes into setting it up. Younger children will probably appreciate having a smaller list and a tighter search area. You could also create a scavenger hunt for a forest or a park, filling it with natural items.

MATERIALS NEEDED:

- A list of the items for which the children will search
- A bag for the children to place their items inside

INSTRUCTIONS:

1. There are two ways to perform this exercise. Should you choose to allow your group to venture into a natural area (like a park, forest, or garden), then the list of items needed should look something like an acorn, a cicada's exoskeleton, a leaf that a bug has bitten, a wildflower, etc.,). Try to comprise the list of items that are not super easy to find but are also not too challenging.
    a. Performing this activity in a smaller and more familiar space means that your list should change to reflect this option (crayon, picture of an author, something gold-colored, a magnet, etc.).
2. Setting up a scavenger hunt in a more natural area is perfect for older children.

OBSERVATION

a. Familiar places make excellent searching areas for smaller kids.

49) QUIET TIME

This is a simple activity that can be an excellent means to expand upon a peaceful mindset. Be sure not to use this exercise as a punishment, or it may lose its utility. Find a day when your children are already feeling peaceful and calm to begin this short observational game.

MATERIALS NEEDED:

- A timer, hourglass, or stopwatch

INSTRUCTIONS:

1. Set the time from one to three minutes and ask the children to be very quiet during this time.

    a. Participants in this activity should be asked to limit their movement, so they are better able to observe the world around them.

2. When the timer goes off, or the hourglass is empty, ask the children what they observed during that time.

3. Challenge the children to maintain the peace they feel into their next activity.

50) TEXTURE CRAFTING

Have you ever wanted an excuse to use a little of your creative prowess? Children are always looking for a way to manifest their imagination. Join them in this activity and use the tools at your disposal to have fun alongside those you are teaching.

Part of learning to observe is taking advantage of the small joys offered by every sense. The nuances of touch and sight can be appreciated through art and the process of creating art. For this activity, you and the participating children are going to spend time creating your own masterpieces and enjoying all of the sensations you experience along the way.

To enjoy this activity, you are not required to get everything on the list below. It would be a good idea to include playdoh or modeling clay, for the strange texture. Pick and choose what items you would like to make available for the children you are crafting alongside.

MATERIALS NEEDED:

- Modeling clay or playdoh
- Assorted string (or yarn)
- Beads (Optional)
- Glitter
- Glue
- Paint and brushes
- Construction paper

OBSERVATION

- Foam sheets
- Pipe cleaners
- Pom poms
- Googly eyes
- Popsicle sticks
- Child-safe scissors
- Markers, crayons, and colored pencils
- Paper plates
- Hole-punch

INSTRUCTIONS:

1. Set apart a block of time to mindfully craft. Observe the unique sensations and textures associated with the available mediums.
2. Instruct every child that they are free to create whatever they like, as long as they are observing the activity with all of their senses.
    a. Do the crayons have a scent?
    b. How does it feel as the wax glides across the page?
    c. What was the texture of the modeling clay?
    d. How does the paint feel as it is brushed across a blank page?
    e. What was your favorite colored Marker?
3. For those who cannot decide on their craft, I will include suggestions below:

a. Popsicle house

b. Sun visor made of paper plate and string

c. Painting of favorite pet

d. Clay sculpture of yourself

e. A comic book about a favorite animal

f. Dream catcher

g. Clay gift for parent (heart, small container, etc.)

51) THE COLORED CARD GAME

This exercise will test the memory of the participating children. They may beat the challenge through observation and focus. This activity requires a little set-up, but your efforts will be worth it.

MATERIALS NEEDED:

- Black and colored construction paper
- Glue
- Scissors
- Sealable plastic bag

Before the game can begin, you must create the cards. This is going to be a memory game based upon sequence. There are a few different ways to make the deck, but you can adjust the directions to your own needs.

OBSERVATION

Cut thick black construction paper into notecard sized pieces. Pick four different colors, other than the black (they should be different shades). Cut one square of each color, two by two inches (the dimensions don't matter, but they can't be close to the edge of the black card).

Glue the colorful squares onto the center of the black cards, making sure that the color comes nowhere near the edges. To skip the hassle of assembly, borrow four cards of differing colors from an Uno deck.

INSTRUCTIONS:

1. Instruct the kids to sit in a circle.
2. The children are going to take turns drawing from the four-card deck in your hand and laying them down in the order that they are removed.
3. The first person to draw with put their cards on the ground for the rest of the group to see. Every child should try to memorize the color order.
4. The cards are shuffled and placed in the center of the circle.
5. The child who just drew the order now picks the person who will try to flip and then place the colored cards in the correct order.
    a. The drawer picks the next person to keep the selection random, so no one knows when they are going to be called upon.

b. The first two people are now ineligible to be selected again until the next round (to keep the game fair).

52) CUP GAME

The Cup Game is a classic party favorite and can be used to challenge the sense of sight and memory. The child watches as you place a ball or pom-pom beneath one cup, in a row of three. You will then shuffle around the cups and then ask the child which one houses the object.

MATERIALS NEEDED:

- Three plastic cups (opaque and not transparent)
- A ball or pom-pom

INSTRUCTIONS:

1. Lay the three cups out in a line.
2. Place the ball or object beneath one of the cups while the children watch.
3. Switch the position of the cups, changing their order.
4. Challenge the child to pick the cup that they believe the object rests beneath.
   a. If you are playing this game with multiple children, have them break into pairs to challenge one another with the cups.

OBSERVATION

53) OBSERVATIONAL MEDITATION

This meditation will teach children the importance of experiencing the world around them with all of their senses. You will guide little ones along an adventure that promises to excite and educate the participating kids. This activity will also make use of your audience's incredible imagination.

Bring a sweet-scented floral candle to light (sneakily) during the meditation to better engage the children in their surroundings. Pick a quiet room where you will be able to dim the lights for this activity. Instruct the children to sit on the floor with their legs crossed in front of them.

THE SCRIPT:

Close your eyes. I want you to listen to the sound of your own breathing and my voice. You may let every other distraction fall away from you. You have no other responsibilities, and nowhere else you are supposed to be at this moment.

Take a few deep breaths before we begin. Allow the world to just melt away as you exhale. You are letting go of more and more tension. Your body is becoming heavy, where it touches the floor.

Take a big breath in and hold it for a count of four before releasing it. As I am talking, do these three more times. When you have finished, you may return to your typical breathing pattern.

Imagine that you are standing in the middle of a vacant stone castle. The rock is weathered and cracked, and part of the roof is entirely missing. Still, the abandoned structure is beautiful. You wonder who used to live here and when they left.

You have no shoes on. As you walk along the stone floor, your feet are chilled by the rock. The sensation sends a shiver up your spine as you continue walking.

The old castle is hauntingly beautiful. Everything is falling apart, but you can tell that this was once a place of importance. There were once people dancing along with these floors in gowns made of gold and silk.

The only sound you can hear is that of your footsteps across the stone floor. There is nothing else inside the castle, except for you. Vines of ivy have overtaken the outside walls and draped over on the inside, where the roof is missing.

A very faint sound echoes through the corridors, but you can't seem to figure out from which direction it came. You know that you are safe here; you can feel it in your bones. Still, there is something else in the castle with you, and you must explore.

Another sound rises up from a distant part of the castle. The echoing makes the sound challenging to follow, but you decide that you must try. You begin to walk in that direction.

As you are walking along, use your attention like a laser pointer. Look around at the empty castle. What do you see upon the walls? What do you hear? Can you smell anything? Turn your focus from one area to the next as you traverse the corridors.

OBSERVATION

Can you use your powers of observation to figure out who lived here before? Do you know why they left? Are there portraits of the family hung upon the tattered walls?

Your feet are beginning to get used to the chill of the stone. A gentle breeze blows against your face; it must be coming in through a hole in the walls. You hear the sound again; it's just a little further ahead, you believe.

Focus on the sound to decide precisely the path you should take. Often times, we are forced to rely on our senses to tell us what to do. Focusing on the present moment means opening yourself up to receiving information from all of them.

Observation is so important because it keeps us grounded in the present moment. As we take in information from our senses, our mind stops wandering. It pours all of its abilities into our laser-focused concentration. Learning to look at every situation with the same laser-focus is the secret to success in so many different areas of life.

You hear a clomping sound, and you are baffled. There is a door just up ahead. Suddenly you smell the loveliest scent, like fresh flowers on a spring day. It is coming from just outside!

A horse neighs just out of sight. You run your fingers against the rough stone wall as you walk closer and closer to the open door. You are swallowed by a warm and cozy feeling that wraps around you like your favorite blanket. Excitement wells up inside your heart, and you feel as though it is going to spill over! Something magical is about to happen; you walk around to the open door, and finally, you see what has been making all that noise.

LILIAN FORSTER

Use your imagination; what do you see? What do you smell? Do you feel anything? What sounds are you hearing? What was waiting for you, right outside that door?

Chapter 6
Visualization, Meditation and Breathing

CHAPTER 6
VISUALIZATION

This chapter will focus mostly on meditation and visualization exercises. By learning to clear the mind, children will venture to magical new places they can call upon whenever they need it. Your voice will guide them to new places made for relaxation and de-stressing.

54) ENCHANTED FOREST

Our first exercise will take children through an enchanted forest. This activity can be used to find stillness on a stimulating day. Participating children will create their own world based around your narration as they learn about themselves, letting their tension fall away.

Have participating children shake the extra energy from their limbs, so they are better able to sit still and listen. Instruct your audience to sit with their legs crossed in front of them; their hands may rest comfortably in their laps. Direct the kids to use their imagination throughout this exercise.

VISUALIZATION

Following this activity, you may have the children draw what they saw at the end of the exercise (if they are comfortable doing so). There are a few elements that the kids design themselves. Bringing those images to life will make it much easier to return to their dreamworld, whenever they please.

THE SCRIPT:

Close your eyes and take a few deep breaths, just like we have practiced before. Inhale through your nose and hold the air inside for a count of four before breathing out through your mouth in a steady stream. Listen only to the sound of my voice and your own breathing.

Throughout this exercise, your mind may begin to wander. It is usual for thoughts to make their way into your head. Remember to accept these feelings and distractions, and then return your attention to our meditation.

You may now return to your regular breathing pattern. Allow all of your muscles to relax a little more with every exhale. You are getting rid of all of your stress and tension, is it just melting away.

There is nothing else that you need to be doing right now. Nowhere else that you need to be. You are entirely safe and free to use your imagination.

I want you to imagine that you are in a beautiful magic forest, right around dusk. You can look up through the leaves of the trees and see that the sky is the loveliest shade of lavender, a pale purple. As the wind blows, you hear rustling all around you and smell the sweet scent of new flowers.

You walk along a path in this forest, knowing that you are entirely safe here. Birds chirp in the distance—boldly colored flowers and blooming all around you, swaying in the night breeze.

There is a distracting rustling to your side. Use your attention like it is a flashlight, shining it on one area and giving that your full concentration. You look around to find the source of the sound.

An adorable rabbit with large eyes and a fluffy tale hops onto the path. The animal seems to want you to follow, so you begin to walk behind the bunny. You are no longer walking along a path.

You trail the rabbit as it glides around twisting trees and over boulders. Look at the forest around you right now. What do you see?

There is a small bride up just ahead. As you approach it, the scent of damp wood fills your nostrils. You cautiously follow your new bunny friend over the sturdy bridge, which still creaks as you walk. The cold lumber is smooth beneath your hands.

The rabbit then dashed ahead, as you make your way through the forest behind him. The animal has brought you to a clearing. The twilight sky is beginning to darken, but the moon is providing plenty of light for your nighttime romp through the trees.

The golden moon shines her light down upon the clearing. You can't believe your eyes as you stand there. Your rabbit friend has led you to paradise.

The clearing in front of you has the most beautiful scene you have ever witnessed. It is precisely what you would consider being perfect. Take a few moments to explore the clearing, knowing that you are entirely safe and comfortable here.

VISUALIZATION

Use your imagination to fill the clearing with detail. Are there beautiful glowing flowers? Mushrooms that look like candy might catch your eye. Perhaps the trees are swaying as they sing a lovely song. Maybe there is a cottage here.

Maybe there is a stunning hot spring surrounded by large rocks. Perhaps you see a waterfall filling a pond. Fireflies could illuminate your new spot. The possibilities are endless.

What sounds do you hear in this paradise? Can you smell anything as the wind is blowing against your cheeks? What colors jump out at you from your clearing?

Take a couple more minutes to use your imagination. Indulge in the paradise that you have created. Allow yourself to surrender to the world inside of you, as all your worries fall away. You are the author of this story.

55) PICTURE OF PARADISE (OPTIONAL)

MATERIALS NEEDED:

- Paper
- Pencil
- Crayons/colored pencils/markers
- Glue (optional)
- Glitter (optional)

INSTRUCTIONS:

1. This is a follow-up activity for meditation. Children can create an illustration of the world they saw inside their heads (at the clearing).
    a. If children uncomfortable sharing the details of their visualization, have them draw the rabbit that guided them along the journey.
2. (Optional) Have the children decorate their drawing with color and glitter.
3. There are no wrong pictures for this activity; the children are merely bringing their imagination to life.
4. Keeping their imagination on-hand will allow kids to return to their paradise whenever they feel tense or stressed out.

56) A MEADOW IN SPRINGTIME

This quick visualization may be accompanied by calming classical music, but no sound is necessary. A Meadow in Springtime will allow children to relax after exercise or other exciting activities while learning about the transient nature of the world. The sound of your voice will encourage their young minds to build a world of splendor and beauty.

Instruct the children to find a position in which they are comfortable. Your audience could rest in a chair, at a desk, or sitting on the ground with their legs crossed in front of them. Direct the kids to allow their hands to fall into their lap.

VISUALIZATION

THE SCRIPT:

Close your eyes as we take a few deep breaths together. We are going to breathe in through our nose to a count of three. Hold the air inside your chest and stomach while you count to four. Exhale in a steady stream to a count of three. We are going to repeat this cycle five times.

Breathe in. Hold it. Breathe out.

Breathe in. Hold it. Breathe out.

Breathe in. Hold it. Breathe out.

Breathe in. Hold it. Breathe out.

Breathe in. Hold it. Breathe out.

You may now return to your typical breathing pattern as we try to relax completely. I want you to remember that should your thoughts wander; you should accept the intrusion and then redirect your attention to the exercise. It is entirely normal to feel fidgety or for your mind to run away occasionally.

Imagine that you are in a meadow surrounded by fresh spring flowers. There are so many magnificent blooms around you, and the air smells sweet (like honeysuckle). The wind is blowing gently, and you feel the breeze lightly disturbing your hair.

Use your senses to try to engage with your meadow. See the beautiful colors and feel the slight wind. Smell all of the dazzling flowers.

You look up to see a clear blue sky with only a few clouds. The sun is shining bright, smiling down upon you and the field. You feel as though you have been wrapped up tight in a warm fuzzy blanket.

You lay down in the grass, and it feels like a luxurious mattress. There is no itching and no dampness, only delightful warm cushion. You could fall asleep here if you wanted, but instead, you watch the clouds as they are slowly flying by.

The spring is one of the most beautiful seasons, so full of life and rebirth. Can you believe that everything was barren only a few months ago? All the flowers that were dead and dull have come back to life in a magnificent display.

Nature works in cycles. There are always going to be dark days (like the winter) and then moments of beauty and rebirth. This pattern repeats in every aspect of the universe; there is terrible so that there can be good.

Our lives behave just like the seasons. There are moments when everything goes wrong, and you can't seem to catch a break. These phases are only temporary, just like the winter. If you weather the ugliness, your entire world will turn back into spring.

Listen to the sound of your breathing as a few birds chirp in the distance. The meadow seems to sway in the breeze as though it is dancing to a beautiful melody. So much light and love surround you. You are loved. You are safe. You are important.

The clouds are shifting overhead. They are your thoughts. Are there any worries that you would like to get rid of? Is there anything about your life that you would like to change?

Allow your troubles to take the form of the clouds over your head. Have you been worried about a friendship? Have you worried about your schoolwork? If so, just place these fears into the fluffy clouds overhead.

VISUALIZATION

Watch as one-by-one; the fluffy clouds begin to disappear. They are returning back into the atmosphere, and they are taking your worries with them. Watch as they dissolve in the air.

Sit for a moment in a completely relaxed position. Allow the excess tension to roll right off of you, like water off of a duck's back. There is nothing unpleasant in your world, and there is no need to worry.

Spend a few more minutes soaking in the warm spring air, beautiful blue sky, and the smell of new flowers. You can return here whenever you wish. Remember the next time life hands you more than you feel like you can handle; every single phase will pass.

57) BUTTERFLY GARDEN

During this exercise, children will relax while listening to a lesson about being unique. This meditation can be used as an escape for an exciting day or to teach about the value of personality. Kids will follow your voice through a striking garden filled with bold curiosities.

Finish this visualization with another craft-time to add even more fun to the activity. Ask the children to draw themselves as a butterfly with the supplies available. The kids may keep their illustration to remind them that they are beautiful and unique.

Children may sit on the floor with their legs crossed in front of them, or they may lay on mats (if any are available). Use a quiet room that can be darkened. Close blinds and shut off lights, leaving only minimal illumination.

Instruct the participating children to dance around for a few minutes before the exercise begins, to release any extra energy. This meditation is meant to be relaxing and calming. Direct your audience to close their eyes and get comfortable.

If the children are laying down for this visualization, recommend that they bend their legs at the knees; their feet should be planted on the ground in this position. Arms will still rest at their sides. Kids who are seated may rest their hands in their lap.

THE SCRIPT:

Close your eyes as we begin this visualization. We are going to start as we always do by taking a few deep breaths to clear our minds. Listen to the sound of the air entering through your nostrils and leaving through your mouth.

Pull the air deep down inside, so that your stomach and chest both expand when you inhale. Hold your breath inside while you count to four, before releasing it. We are going to repeat these steps for five cycles.

Breathe the air in for a count of three, holding it for a count of four. Breathe out to a count of three.

Breathe in while you count to three in your head, hold it for four, and then release.

Inhale the air as you count to three again. Listen to your breath and the sound of my voice. Hold and release.

Breathe the air deep down inside you, hold and then release.

Inhale and feel your stomach expanding. Hold the air for a count of four before breathing out.

VISUALIZATION

Imagine that you are standing inside a spectacular garden. There are so many different flowers blooming all around you. An array of colors and shapes!

The area looks a little like a small maze. Walls of vines and trees keep prying eyes away from the precious beauty. A small pond in the center of the garden is faintly glowing blue. There is so much shade created from the cozy walls of plants and ivy.

There is a gentle rain coming down upon you, but you don't mind. The water is slightly chilly. Moisture nourishes the plants and helps to grow the beautiful flowers. They all seem to appreciate the mist.

The drizzle also makes the garden look even more beautiful and adds mystery. You can hear the gentle tapping of the rain against the leaves as you walk around. Smell the various scents coming from all of the flowers mixed with that of damp trees.

This is not just any old garden, though. This is a magical place, shaded by trees, and kept secret from the eyes of the public. You are the first person to ever find this whimsical lot, and the flowers kept here have never seen a person before. They sway and dance in delight as you pass.

The rain begins to stop, and the sun is coming back out. Slowly, all of the flowers are bathed in a soft light that somehow makes it through all of the trees and their leaves. Steam rises up from the ground because of all the moisture in the air.

The glorious colors look even more magnificent in the light of the sun. You can see all of the details. There are so many different flowers scattered all around the winding garden. Everywhere you look, there are new shapes and hues to behold.

Lovely purple flowers that are shaped like upside-down bells have caught the rain for their thirsty stems. Pink daisies bounce around in the wind. There are crimson roses that look as though they have been splashed with white paint, hiding in a corner.

Something magical seems to be happening all around you. The air is filling with glitter and blue dust. As the flowers begin to dry off, they are moving more and more. Before, it seemed as though they were just being tossed about by the wind. Now they appear to be alive.

Brilliantly glowing blooms, glittering blooms, neon blooms, they all seem to be moving a twitching in the soft breeze. Then it happens! One of the flowers flies free of its stem. '

All of the magical blooms are turning into butterflies! The most elegant and stunning butterflies anyone has ever seen. The air seems to be filled with an electric sort of enchantment, as plants all around start to come to life.

Watch the rainbow world breathing as it comes to life. You find yourself amazed. You are so surprised by the unbelievable change that you do not even notice that something is happening to you, at first. Your limbs are starting to feel light.

You are turning into a magnificent butterfly. Your body is shrinking as the transformation takes place. Beautiful wings are sprouting from your back. Your legs have turned into small black limbs, able to grip the stems of plants.

What colors are your wings? Are they sparkling? Do your butterfly wings glow?

VISUALIZATION

You begin to feel the cool air surrounding your body as you flap your magnificent wings. The motion is lifting you from the ground; your legs are dangling beneath you. You are flying.

You have never felt so light or so free. Your entire body feels weightless as the breeze carries you along. The other butterflies slow down so that you can catch up to them.

Every butterfly in the garden is so unique and beautiful, including you. You all have different patterns and colors of your wings. Each of you has something that makes you special and unique.

Some butterflies have swirls on their wings, while others have diamonds, stripes, spots, and other abstract shapes. Some wings are golden, and others are transparent! There are long wings, short wings, lacey wings, and regular wings.

You are gliding through the air as you make your way around the garden. You see more and more butterflies. The enchanted garden is rich with magic.

You flip through the air before turning upside-down. You make an extraordinary butterfly! You are different from every single other living creature. Everything about you is striking, unique, and magnificent.

Find a nice branch to rest on while you say goodbye to the garden and all of your new friends. Don't worry; you can return here whenever you like. Come visit this enchanted paradise again the next time you need a little reminder that you are special and beautiful in your own unique way.

58) PICTURE OF MY WINGS

MATERIALS NEEDED:

- Paper (or canvas)
- Pencil
- Paint (optional)
- Crayons, markers, or colored pencils (optional)
- Glue (optional)
- Glitter (optional)
- Pipe cleaners, pom poms, foam sheets, miscellaneous art supplies (optional)

INSTRUCTIONS:

1. Direct the participating children to draw a picture of themselves as butterflies.
    a. If the children are too young, create a butterfly template for them.
2. Instruct the kids to color and design their butterfly to look how it did in their visualization meditation.
3. Allow the children to keep their image to remind them that they are special and unique, just as each butterfly was one of a kind!

VISUALIZATION

59) CABIN MEDITATION

In the following visualization, children will be made to feel comfortable and cozy. By listening to your voice, they will take a vacation to a faraway place. This exercise can be utilized at any time and will be especially helpful for reducing stress before a taxing activity.

Pick a quiet room where you will not be disturbed. The sound of your voice should be audible. Dim the lights for a more relaxing tone.

Make sure that your audience has gotten all of their excess energy out before the exercise begins. Instruct the children to sit on the floor with their legs crossed in front of them. Participants may allow their hands to fall into a comfortable position on their lap.

THE SCRIPT:

Close your eyes and listen to the sound of my voice and the noise of your breathing. We are going to take several deep breaths to ready the body and clear the mind. I would like for you to draw the air all the way down into our stomach. Feel your belly expand as you inhale and hold your breath for a count of four.

Count to three each time you inhale and exhale. We are going to take five deep breaths, and then you may return to your regular pattern. We are inhaling to a count of three, holding for a count of four, and then exhaling to a count of three. Ready?

Inhale for a count of three. Hold while you count to four. Exhale to a count of three.

Inhale again, hold for a count of four and then exhale.

Repeat this, breathing in for a count of three. Hold the air in your belly for a count of four and then breathe out.

Breathe in again, hold the air, and then exhale.

One last time, we are breathing in for a count of three. Hold the air inside you while you count to four and then release it as you count to three.

You may now return to your regular breathing pattern. Continue to listen to the sound of the air moving through you as we go along. Should you find your thoughts straying, just redirect them back to the visualization.

Imagine that you have just found yourself inside a beautiful little cabin at the top of a big mountain. You look outside a window to see the snow-capped peaks covered in giant cone-shaped pine trees. The glass in front of you is fogging up from your breath; it looks so cold outside.

The limbs of the pine trees are all covered in snow and ice. The ground directly outside is pure white and undisturbed. Fresh flakes are falling from the heavens, still adding more and more layers to the already blanketed ground.

The wilderness outside looks like a winter wonderland, so untamed and fragile. You watch as a bright red cardinal appears in the snow, leaving little holes behind him. He is hunting for seeds.

The inside of the cabin is warm and safe. A fireplace has heated the small wooden home, making the building cozy and comfortable. You sit on the luxuriously fluffy couch, in front of you rests a mug of hot chocolate.

VISUALIZATION

Every sip of cocoa warms your insides and makes you feel like singing. You decide that the time has come to explore outside. You put on your most massive coat and snow gear before wandering through the front door. You cross a rustic front porch and make your way into the mountain yard.

The snow crunches beneath your shoes as you walk. Light specks of ice land on your nose and throughout your hair; the flurries are covering you. You keep walking along, observing all of the beauty.

You take some time to play in the snow. Your gloves and coat are entirely protecting you from the elements, and you feel delightful. When you have finished building snowmen, you return to the front porch to watch the flurries continue to fall. There is a line of rocking chairs from which to choose.

The falling snow makes light taps against the surfaces it lands upon. So many flakes have fallen that your tracks are already gone. You smile as you rock back and forth, enjoying the peace.

60) SPIRIT CREATURE

The following exercise will allow children a chance to use their imagination throughout a short meditation. Your little ones may use the insight they gain from this visualization to infer new things about themselves. Curious young minds will love the chance to assess themselves through the lens of their own creativity.

Direct the children to shake out their excess energy before you begin. Instruct the participating audience to sit with their legs crossed in front of them and their hands resting in their lap. You may choose to dim the room to create a more relaxing environment, but it is not necessary to do so.

THE SCRIPT:

Close your eyes and take a few deep breaths as you listen to the sound of my voice and the noise the air makes as it travels through you. We want to breathe in through our nose and then out through our mouth, holding the air inside for a count of three. After a few of these, you may return to your regular pattern.

Inhale through your nose and hold it for a moment before exhaling through your mouth. Repeat this breath again, holding and then releasing. One more time, take a very deep breath and feel it in your belly before exhaling through your mouth.

I want you to imagine that you are in a beautiful cave. Lanterns inside the cavern have illuminated it so that you can see in front of you. The sides of the structure are made of shiny black rock.

There are words and images etched into the black stone. Each of the craved symbols is glowing, your favorite color. In the center of the cavern, there is a small pool of water that is also glowing your favorite color.

You notice that the carvings on the walls of the cave are related to you. There are images of the things you like and words that relate to your friends, family, and interests. Each symbol corresponds to an essential part of your life! You have never seen anything like this before.

VISUALIZATION

The walls are so beautiful and so meaningful; it is as though the deepest parts of your mind are on display in front of you. All of the hobbies that you have ever loved and everything that you are good at is represented in pictures before you. Take a moment and scan the walls of the cave.

The pool behind you has started bubbling and steaming. You cautiously walk over to the liquid. There is a border of stones around the edge of the water.

The closer you get to the pool, the more relaxed you feel. The tension from your muscles is melting away with every step you take. When you are standing right in front of the bubbling water, you feel terrific. Your limbs are light, you have no muscle tension, and it seems as though you could fly away.

You gaze into the pool, and the water begins to calm down. The bubbling stops completely, and you see a familiar face staring back at you from the liquid. Details are becoming more and more visible as the spring stops moving.

The face of the person you love most in the entire world is gazing back at you through the pool. At this moment, you feel entirely safe. There is no worry or stress in your body, at all. A pleasant breeze sweeps your cheek.

You hear a rustling sound behind you, coming from the mouth of the cave. You turn around to see what could possibly be making the noise. There is a beautiful and majestic creature in front of you.

The animal that you meet here is going to be different from everyone else's. The creature standing in front of you is your guardian. You will keep this being inside you, always.

You are meeting the creature tasked with watching you and protecting you. Stay here and study your animal for just a moment more before opening your eyes. Every animal is unique, and you are allowed to draw your own conclusions about your guardian and why that particular being was chosen to watch over you.

Take some time to gather your opinions and assumptions related to the animal that appeared to you and then compare those traits to your own. Example: I saw a dog. I have always believed that dogs were loyal and compassionate, so maybe I am those things too.

61) PICTURE OF YOUR GUARDIAN (OPTIONAL)

This optional activity allows children the chance to express their creativity by drawing the animal that appeared to them within their meditation/visualization. Kids may keep the illustration to remind themselves of their better nature. It can be easy to lose oneself in the noise. The sketch may act as a method for grounding your little one.

MATERIALS NEEDED:

- Paper
- Pencil
- Crayons, colored pencils, markers (optional)

INSTRUCTIONS

1. Have children illustrate the creature that appeared to them in the cave.

VISUALIZATION

2. Kids may keep this image with them, to remind themselves of their true nature and who they really are.

3. The illustration may also give children strength in times of strife or sadness.

Chapter 7
Body and Senses

CHAPTER 7

BODY AND SENSES

One of the most exciting parts of being young is that the mind is in a constant state of discovery. There is no end to the new information as your brain is in the process of developing. This chapter will focus on children's relationship with their physical being. Learning to understand and accept oneself is vital to mindfulness and advancement upon the path of self-discovery.

62) BEATING HEART

In this exercise, children will learn about the function of the heart and the way the organ behaves. Through observation of the resting heart rate and then the stressed heart rate, little ones will have the chance to see their bodies working in real-time. There is nothing quite as fascinating as the human physique.

MATERIALS NEEDED:

- Stopwatch or timer.
- Paper and writing utensils.

INSTRUCTIONS:

1. Direct the participating children to place their index and middle finger on the wrist of their opposite arm, to find their pulse. Place the palm upward and then trace down from the thumb, until their fingertips lay on the outer edge of the wrist.
    a. If a child is unable to find their pulse in this way, have them place the same two fingers on their neck. Should you use this method, trace from the outside corner of the eye, down to the neck (just beneath the jaw).
2. Time the children as they take their pulse for ten seconds, and then multiply their number by six.
    a. If the kids are old enough to count reasonably high, just have them observe their pulse for the full minute for more accurate results.
3. Record the results of the first measurement so that it may be referred to later.
4. Have the children participate in strenuous activity for a few minutes (twenty-five jumping jacks).
5. Immediately upon completion, direct the children to retake their pulse.

BODY AND SENSES

6. Have the children compare the first result with the second to note what should be a massive difference.

Why does your pulse increase during and after exercise? (Script)

There are two elementary principals about the human body that you must understand before this explanation. The is responsible for pumping blood out to all of our limbs. The lungs are our breathing equipment; the organ takes in oxygen so that we can survive.

You have probably noticed from all of the breathing exercises that the human body loves oxygen. Air is the electricity that powers our machine. The element becomes even more powerful when our muscles are working harder.

Oxygen is transported throughout the body, in our blood. When we jump around, our muscles require much more oxygen to properly do their job. The heart pumps faster so that it can send out all of the restorative materials with more speed.

The blood travels by the lungs, making a pitstop to pick up all the oxygen it needs to properly nourish the muscles. You may have noticed that exercise also causes us to breathe heavier; it is because we need additional air to function. The lungs work harder to bring the oxygen in, and the heart works harder to distribute it.

63) FLAMINGO

This is another exercise focused on helping the children understand their own bodies. Balance is a skill that so many of us still struggle with. Test the participating kid's abilities by asking them to engage in the following activity.

INSTRUCTIONS:

1. Ask the participating children to stand on one leg.
2. Tell them to find something in the room to stare at, fixing their sight upon the point.
3. As your group is trying to balance, ask the kids questions that are unrelated to the task at hand. You could also play music or maybe start a game of catch with a soft (as in squishy) ball.
4. Tell the children to observe how difficult balancing becomes when their minds are otherwise occupied.

Why did balancing become more difficult? (Script)

Humans have a limited amount of brainpower available for use at any given moment. Balancing takes a lot of concentration and self-control, even though it may seem like a simple task. If you are sleepy or you begin to divide your attention between other things, the mind's power becomes used up.

For you to maintain your stance on one leg, your brain has to do a lot of work. You actually have an organ just for balancing inside your ear. Your mind is working with information from your eyes, muscles, and the balance organ to keep you from falling over.

BODY AND SENSES

64) STOP

The STOP exercise is another activity devoted to balancing. You will need plenty of room for your participants to move around. Children will love this game-style lesson, and it will teach them more about movement and the utility of their own bodies.

The game involves playing music that is stopped intermittently, as the children freeze alongside the pauses and try to hold their position for five to ten seconds. STOP is sure to produce a lot of laughs. This activity is also useful to rid children of excess energy.

MATERIALS NEEDED:

- A device with which to play music
- Your phone works just fine, as long as you can stop and resume the tunes quickly.

INSTRUCTIONS:

1. Set-up the device that you will use to play music
2. Instruct the children to dance (or just flail about) to the song until you stop the sound without warning for five to ten seconds.
3. The object of the game is to freeze in place when the music is paused.

4. The children will learn more about balance and movement as they struggle to maintain difficult positions that were easily achieved while in motion.

65) TASTE TEST

In this exercise, your child will be exercising their senses through a taste-test. Pick some food items that the children are acquainted with, but not things that they are exposed to every single day. You will blindfold the participants, and then instruct them to taste and subsequently guess the food they are experiencing.

MATERIALS NEEDED:

- Seven to ten items of food or candy with an exciting texture, smell, taste, etc
- Be sure to have enough items for all children participating in the activity.
- Blindfolds
- Plates
- Cups (if you are using and liquids)

INSTRUCTIONS:

1. Blindfold every child participating in the exercise at one time (or bring a different selection for each kid).

BODY AND SENSES

2. Set the food items on plates and organize them in front of the children, in the order they will be tasting.
3. Instruct the children to taste the first item in front of them.
   a. When they are tasting their item, ask them to pay attention to the way the food smells and its texture. Using their senses, they should attempt to identify the mystery food/candy/drink.
4. Ask the children guiding questions about the experience.
   a. Have you noticed anything new about this food?
   b. Does it have the same taste when you are blindfolded?
   c. How is the smell changing your experience?
   d. Does using your senses make the experience better or worse?
5. When you have finished with the first item, move on to the next. Repeat steps three and four for everything, asking questions along the way.

When this challenge is completed, children should have a renewed understanding of the way our senses can alter our perception. Studies have shown that watching television while eating causes a reduction in taste. Our brain cannot process incoming information while receiving complete data from the tastebuds.

By using a blindfold, not only are children tasked with using their senses to identify the food item, but they are also tasting the most complete version of a dish they likely consume regularly. It can be fascinating to observe the way the loss of sight can change our perception. Taste, touch, and smell are often heightened in the absence of visual stimuli.

66) BRAVE OLD WORLD

In this activity, you and your participants will take a new look at the area where you spend the most time together. The children will wear a blindfold while examining a place they thought they knew. Can they rely on their senses to tell them where they are? Or will everything seem utterly different without the benefit of sight?

MATERIALS NEEDED:

- Blindfold

INSTRUCTIONS:

1. Have the children go one at a time if you are working with more than one child.
2. Blindfold the child who will be going first.
3. Spin the participant around in circles as they stand. This works to disorient those wearing the blindfold.
4. Instruct the blindfolded child to walk around the classroom/home. Direct them to reach out and feel the space around them as they try to answer the following questions:
    a. Where are you?
    b. What are you touching?

c. Do you notice anything new that you didn't pick up on when you could see?

   d. What direction is the entrance to the room from where you are now?

   e. Can you go to (name feature of the room)?

67) RED LIGHT GREEN LIGHT

This beloved childhood game can be used to test observational and motor skills, as kids screech to a halt to avoid being sent back to the starting line. There is a strategy to this game, which may or may not reveal itself to the kids. Needless to say, this exercise requires a lot of space. The activity is better used when more than one child is participating.

The game will start off with you calling the movements. If enough children are participating, then the winner can take over that role during subsequent rounds. The person calling the movements stands across the room or field from the players.

INSTRUCTIONS:

1. If you are playing outside, mark off two lines that give you a large area to play the game. If you are playing inside, then have the participating children along the opposite wall from where you will stand.

2. Everyone is stationary until you call "green light" and turn (facing away) from the children. Wait a moment before calling "red light" and turning back around.

3. Anyone who is still in motion when you turn back around will return to their starting position at the opposite side of the room.

4. The first participant to make it all the way over to you wins the game. If enough participants are playing, they may be the caller for the next round.

This game necessitates that the children listen and can stop in time to avoid being caught. To win this game, children will have to use a steady speed instead of running as quickly as they can. Participants who advance too quickly will have a difficult time stopping by the time you turn around.

68) OBSTACLE COURSE

Setting up an obstacle course is a relatively simple and super fun way to acquaint children with their motor skills. You may use the items in your house (couch and cushions, pillows, end tables, chairs) to create your challenges, or you can buy items from the store (boxes, boards, hula hoops, balls). A good combination of both could make for a fantastic course.

MATERIALS NEEDED SUGGESTED:

- Hula hoops
- Chairs

BODY AND SENSES

- Boards
- Couch
- Cushions
- Laundry basket
- Beanbag Chair
- Boxes
- Bricks
- Balls
- Tables
- Pillows
- Pool Noodles

COURSE SUGGESTIONS:

- Instruct participants to throw a large beanbag chair into a round lattice laundry basket.
- Use two sturdy objects of the same height (like bricks) to act as the base for a balancing board.
- Have participants crawl beneath a chair or table.
- A ring toss set can be purchased to add a little flair to the obstacle course.
- The string may be tied to two surfaces to make a limbo pole.

YOGA FOR CHILDREN

The following activity consists of a few specific yoga poses that may be accomplished by children. Yoga has long been a way to achieve mindfulness and ground yourself to the present moment. Watch your little one's mind begin to surrender to peace as they practice maintaining these stances.

69) PRAYER POSE

This is a stance that is typically used at the beginning of a session or class. Teach your little ones to stand straight with their hands meeting in front of them (at chest level) as though they are praying. The prayer pose would be a perfect first step for learning yoga.

70) CHAIR POSE

Instruct children to raise their arms into the air (straight) and then bend their knees as if they are sitting in an invisible chair. This is a more advanced move than the prayer pose but does not require the legs to make a ninety-degree angle.

Imagine a chair that is tipping forward. Feet will point forward, and the chest remains straight. Thighs should be almost parallel with the floor (but not entirely).

BODY AND SENSES

71) LUNGE POSE

The lunge pose requires participants to lunge to the front, kicking their opposite leg out behind them. The back leg should form a straight line, while the arms rest alongside the front leg (which is bent in a ninety-degree angle). The child's hands may lay on the floor, supporting their stance.

72) WARRIOR POSE

From the lunge pose, bring the torso and arms up until they are perpendicular to the floor. The child's arms and torso should be vertical (but still facing forward), while the legs remain bent in the lunge position.

73) WARRIOR II

From the Warrior pose, allow the arms to fall until they are horizontal (parallel to the floor). The torso twists to the left-hand side, while the bottom half of the body remains the same. The top half of the body should form the better "t."

74) BODY ACCEPTANCE CRAFT

In the following activity, children will create a visual reminder that their body is essential and beautiful, just the way it is. Younger children may need your assistance when it comes to the writing portion of the craft. This exercise allows for that beautiful childhood imagination to flourish.

MATERIALS NEEDED:

- Construction Paper
- Pencil
- Colored pencils

INSTRUCTIONS:

1. Instruct each child to come up with five things they love about themselves; one of the entries must give thanks to their body.
2. The children will then trace one of their hands on a piece of light-colored paper.
3. One of their reasons should be written inside each of their fingers (on the paper).
4. The children may then use colored pencils to decorate their pictures with things that relate to the reasons that they choose.
   a. If the child picked being kind as a reason for loving themselves, they could decorate their picture with hearts.
   b. If the child said they liked their hair, they could draw hairbows.

Reasons to Love Your Body

- You are so tall that you can reach everything!
- You are so short that you can sneak around without being caught.
- You have great hair.

BODY AND SENSES

- You are strong.
- You can run really fast.
- You have a friendly smile.
- You give the best hugs.
- You have a fantastic memory.
- Your eye color is really pretty.

Reasons to Love Yourself

- You are kind.
- You are an excellent singer.
- You are brilliant.
- You have a great sense of humor.
- You have so my fun.
- You love to learn.
- You are super good at math.
- You are a sharp dresser.
- You are really creative.
- Your imagination is so vivid.
- You have an extensive vocabulary.
- You are protective of others.
- You never give up on your dreams.
- You know that you have a bright future.
- You are good at making friends.

- You make people laugh.
- You are a good friend.

75) A THANK YOU NOTE (MEDITATION)

This exercise is meant to help children learn to love themselves and their bodies. Through listening to this relaxing meditation, little ones will hopefully look at their incredible limbs with appreciation. We put our body through so much, and it faithfully carries us forward.

Instruct the children to sit with their legs crossed in front of them or lying down upon mats (if they are available). Turn down the lights so participants can concentrate without being distracted by their surroundings.

THE SCRIPT:

Close your eyes and listen to the sound of my voice. I want you to take a few deep breaths to clear your mind. Breathe in through your nose and out through your mouth. Pull the air all the way down into your belly and hold it there for just a moment before releasing it.

Take another deep breath in through your nose and out through your mouth. As you are breathing, your muscles are relaxing more and more. The places on your body that are touching the ground are beginning to feel heavier as you un-tense your muscles and follow along to the sound of my voice.

Today we are going to talk about your body and the way it works for you. Your body is a fantastic and beautiful machine that does its best to carry you around. You are perfect, no matter your size, height,

BODY AND SENSES

shape, or ability. You have precisely the form that you were meant to have.

The entire human body is made of cells. All of these tiny organic machines all work together to keep you alive. When you decide that you want to walk across the room or pick up an object, your physical form makes sure that you are able.

Bring your awareness to your feet. You may have long toes or short toes. You may even have crooked toes that can't decide between being long or short. Every single toe is beautiful. It is a small part of a great machine that runs only for you. Your toes team up with your feet to transport you wherever your brain decides it wants to go. Take a moment to fill your heart with appreciation for your feet and the work they do.

Bring your attention to your knees and legs. There are so many different kinds of legs! Your particular legs are a work of art that only exists to make sure you are mobile. Those legs coordinate with your mind and your feet to take you from one place to another, and for that, they deserve a sweet "thank you."

Whenever you find yourself comparing your body to someone else's, stop. You are perfect and beautiful, and your body was made for you. You are the only one allowed to have your body, and growing to love it will bring so much happiness into your young life. Comparison is poisonous and will pollute your mind.

People all around you will worry over their bodies. You will know that all of you are a work of art. There is no one else who looks like you, and you are lovely just the way you are.

LILIAN FORSTER

Everyone is filled with doubt about their looks because the world we live in encourages that doubt. Some people see every single trait that separates them from the bland average as a flaw. Freckles are a flaw. Large teeth are a flaw. Crooked toes, boney legs, and love handles are not flaws. The things that set us apart should be celebrated.

You can decide what is beautiful for yourself. You have the power to accept and embrace yourself. Learning to love your body for the spectacular machine that it is will bring you peace.

There are so many vital organs just below your stomach, and they are all working to make sure that you keep functioning. Your lungs and heart are distributing blood and oxygen to every single limb so that you can achieve your dreams. Think of your beautiful shoulders and the weight they have held. Think of all the places this body will take you.

Your arms, which move on command, have hugged so many of the people you love. They deserve your thanks. Your hands, which have felt the world around you, write letters and draw pictures. They also deserve appreciation.

Your neck has one of the most important jobs, holding up your head. Your great head and the ever-dreaming brain that rests inside of it are always working to achieve your goals. Allow yourself to feel thankful for the perfect body that you have been given and for all the places it will take you.

CONCLUSION

Congratulations! You have made it to the end of *Mindfulness Exercises for Kids: 75 Relaxation Techniques to Help Your Child Feel Better.* I hope that this book has provided you and your children with hours of educational entertainment. You may use these exercises for years to come. Learning about mental and emotional health does not have to be dull and colorless.

Childhood is such a developmentally significant period in human life. The information that we take in while we are young forms our habits and values well into adulthood. Mindfulness is a healthy subject of study for growing brains, offering a sense of peace and a beneficial relationship with the self.

Changing schedules, new social expectations, and an ever-learning mind can make being young a stressful affair. Activities that teach little ones to manage anxiety are almost necessary for the modern era. Growing to accept, understand, and love oneself can drastically change the quality of life as the years roll on. Encouraging emotional maturity in children can ensure that our future leaders are compassionate, empathetic, and understanding.

LILIAN FORSTER

Together we have tackled stress, emotion, self-soothing, bodily awareness, observational skills, and meditation. Controlled breathing and visualization have given your kids the tools they need to handle even the most challenging days. I hope that the children in your life have benefited so much from the time that you have spent together. Return to these activities from time-to-time, to witness all of the profess that has been made.